Praise for
Seizing the Good Life

"I love everything about this Bible study, from hearing Shellie's sweet personal discussions with John, to sharing the Word of God, to her moving prayers—all of which had me in tears throughout the book. It is a reminder that even when we're so busy in life, we must cling to the Truth, the Gospel of Jesus Christ. No matter what comes our way, He is dwelling in us, He will never leave us, and we can find peace in that truth. Several ladies are asking me to host a Bible study, and *Seizing the Good Life* will be in our future."

—**Jessica Robertson,** television personality and author of several books, including *The Women of Duck Commander* and *The Good, the Bad, and the Grace of God*

"In *Seizing the Good Life*, Shellie Rushing Tomlinson offers a refreshingly creative deep dive into the book of John. In these pages, seasoned Bible readers will discover fresh inspiration, and new students of the Bible will find the book of John to be delightfully approachable. Reading like one part Bible study, one part peek into a warm correspondence between friends, each chapter of this book will leave you excited to start the next as you learn from John what it means to have 'life in the power of Jesus's name.'"

—**Monica Swanson,** author of *Boy Mom* and *Raising Amazing*, and host of the *Monica Swanson* podcast

"With an abundance of wit and wisdom, Shellie gives fresh insight into the life-changing power contained in the Gospel of John."

—**Lynne Gentry,** *USA Today* bestselling author

T0035857

"There's a confidence in Shellie Rushing Tomlinson's warmly candid writer's voice that grants both depth and excitement to her journey through John's gospel to rediscover joy and peace as we abide in the living Christ. An original, modern, timely Bible study, *Seizing the Good Life* is a bold invitation to hear in fresh ways all that John records about the One Who gives His all for our most and best."

—**Patricia Raybon,** award-winning author of *I Told the Mountain to Move: Learning to Pray So Things Change* and the *One Year God's Great Blessings Devotional*

"Wow—*Seizing the Good Life* is my new favorite Bible study! I love the way Shellie Rushing Tomlinson dissects the Word of God in her endearingly conversational style, exploring biblical meanings we never knew, and helping us understand the apostle behind the divinely anointed words of his gospel. Shellie paints a fresh portrait of Christ—the man, the God, and the long-awaited Messiah. And as always, her personal stories and comments are spot-on and entertaining as well as encouraging. I hope you'll join me in this exciting journey of discovery of the book of John: listen, learn, and live the Truth as you seize the good life."

—**Debora M. Coty,** event speaker and bestselling author of the *Too Blessed to Be Stressed* series

"Shellie Rushing Tomlinson combines storytelling and Bible teaching in her extraordinary new book *Seizing the Good Life*. It makes me want to go deeper into God's Word. I absolutely love this study and plan to do it with friends!"

—**Jenn Gotzon,** actress, producer, and creator of *The Farmer and The Belle*

"For those who are willing to sit and savor, to read the familiar in a new way, Shellie Rushing Tomlinson will be your guide. Her study of the book of John unfolds from two refreshing angles that lend creativity and personal experience to each passage. The book of John is an intimate window into Jesus's life—and this is a new way to immerse yourself in it."

—**Laurie Polich Short,** author of *Faith, Doubt, and God's Mysterious Timing* and *40 Verses to Ignite Your Faith*

"Shellie has hit a home run and is running the bases with her hands in the air and her heart on the line. *Seizing the Good Life* is real, relatable, and stone-cold honest. From wrangling ugly feelings to jumping for joy, this book has it all. It teaches us to live life fearlessly and faithfully. The message of the book of John is so clearly understood and brought to life in this unique style. What a priceless gem this book is to every person who reads it. A treasure awaits. Dig in!"

—**Tammy Whitehurst,** speaker, humorist, and author of *High Heels and Hallelujahs*

"Nothing the world has to offer can fill us with true joy or lasting peace, but Jesus offers us both in abundance. Shellie Rushing Tomlinson passionately encourages us to pursue Him with abandon so we can fully experience all He wants to give us. With a refreshing blend of scriptural depth and humor, Shellie guides us through the Gospel of John, highlighting pertinent spiritual truths for our journey. Part book and part Bible study, *Seizing the Good Life* is unique, engaging, and well worth your time!"

—**Kathy Howard,** Bible teacher and award-winning author of *Heirloom* and the *Deep Rooted* devotional series

Seizing the Good Life

Seizing the Good Life

Discover Peace and Joy through the Study of John's Gospel

SHELLIE RUSHING TOMLINSON

SALEM
BOOKS

an imprint of Regnery Publishing
Washington, D.C.

Unless otherwise marked, All Scripture quotations are taken from the (NASB®) New American Standard Bible®, Copyright © 1960, 1971, 1977, 1995, and 2020 by the Lockman Foundation. Used by permission. All rights reserved. www.lockman.org

Scriptures marked ESV are taken from ESV® Bible (The Holy Bible, English Standard Version®), Copyright © 2001 by Crossway, a publishing ministry of Good News Publishers. Used by permission. All rights reserved.

Scripture quotations marked (NIV) are taken from the Holy Bible, New International Version®, NIV®. Copyright © 1973, 1978, 1984, 2011 by Biblica, Inc.™ Used by permission of Zondervan. All rights reserved worldwide. www.zondervan.com The "NIV" and "New International Version" are trademarks registered in the United States Patent and Trademark Office by Biblica, Inc.™

Salem Books™ is a trademark of Salem Communications Holding Corporation. Regnery® and its colophon are registered trademarks of Salem Communications Holding Corporation.

Cataloging-in-Publication data on file with the Library of Congress.

ISBN: 978-1-68451-384-0
eISBN: 978-1-68451-438-0

Published in the United States by
Salem Books
An Imprint of Regnery Publishing
A Division of Salem Media Group
Washington, D.C.

www.SalemBooks.com

Manufactured in the United States of America

10 9 8 7 6 5 4 3 2 1

Books are available in quantity for promotional or premium use. For information on discounts and terms, please visit our website: www.SalemBooks.com

To my longtime readers, who graciously indulge my ongoing efforts to wrap words around anything and everything Jesus teaches me. I never tire of offering you my musings. I pray they help you glory in His goodness and stay in full pursuit of Him, too. And to the new friends who will pick up this study, welcome!

We're an imperfect bunch of Jesus-lovers, bonded by shared amazement in His astounding grace, and you're warmly invited to join us. We aim to support you, without comparison or competition, for Jesus is the starting block, the One who runs with us, and the finish line we crave.

Hugs, Shellie

Contents

Introduction

My grandson's shaky little voice joined mine. We used the index fingers of our right hands to draw circles in the darkness while we sang, our fingers barely discernible in the bands of moonlight streaming through the crack in the curtains. It's been a few years since that night, but I well remember feeling the tears on Connor's cheeks as he pressed his face against my own and whispered the lyrics, *"This little light of mine, I'm gonna let it shine…"* Connor and his brother, along with three of their cousins, were at our house for "Pops and Keggie Kamp," an annual extravaganza their granddad and I host here on the banks of Lake Providence, Louisiana.

Kamp is full of water sports, farm explorations, crafting, and snacks. It's built around morning devotions and sprinkled with visits from the great-grandparents. Although Connor had been looking forward to Kamp for months and he'd been all-in during the day's fun-in-the-sun activities, bedtime had brought a swift and unexpected meltdown. Connor missed his mommy.

I found him on my routine round of prayer and snuggles. His enormous brown eyes and quivering lower lip testified of his anxious heart and totally wrecked his Keggie's. Lying on our backs in a guest bedroom, I pulled Connor close and asked if he still wanted to sing "our song." He did.

All our grandchildren have enjoyed singing "This Little Light of Mine" at one time or another during bedtime rituals, but Connor embraces it like no other. Over time, the two of us have developed a habit of singing it with different beats, based on whatever rhythm "Con Con" is feeling at the time. Country, rap, bluesy—I thought we'd performed it in every possible cadence one could imagine, but this was our first time to sing it through hiccups and tears.

"*I won't let Satan blow it out—I'm gonna let it shine…*" Even now, I can see Connor trying to gather himself to expel a good strong puff of breath halfway through that line. It's our custom, and it's meant to illustrate our determination to protect our Jesus lights at all costs. Connor's body was shaking as he sang it.

I don't think I could find a better illustration of what so many of us twenty-first-century believers look like if I tried. We so want to stand firm in our faith, but the world is rocking, and our knees are knocking.

There's no denying it: Satan is bent on blowing out our faith candles, but the glorious news is that he doesn't have to win! Our enemy can huff and puff like the big bad wolf, but he's powerless to blow out the candle Jesus has put in our hearts if we know who Christ is in us and who we are in Him. I've been in a deep dive into the Gospel of John for a while now, and I'm pumped to share what I've been learning with you!

I need to level with you. People these days have a tendency to take an á la carte approach to the Christian faith—picking and choosing the biblical truths they like and ignoring the rest to curate their own personalized religious experience. John has nothing to say to any of us if we're bent on taking our faith apart and trying to build it back into something more comfortable and easier to live with—but he has plenty to teach us about having an ever-growing faith and the real-life challenge of continuing to believe. The apostle's humility is on painful display as he openly documents the disciples' embarrassingly rocky road to believing all that Jesus was teaching them. John records how he and his friends came to believe that Jesus was who He said He was, and how they learned to keep believing in Him even though He wasn't going about His restorative, kingdom-building work in any of the tangible ways they had hoped or expected.

With some of the last words of his gospel, John reveals his reason for writing. He hopes to challenge his readers to believe and keep believing so they can "have life in [Jesus's] name" (John 20:31). Yes and amen. I'm motivated by the same goal.

Does "life in His name" sound good to you? It does to me, but over and again, we're tempted to surrender that promise to a vague suck-it-up-buttercup faith experience instead. Our faces might belie the inner joy we profess to know, but we expect others to trust us when we insist that it's there. I'm calling foul. God wants us to so believe in, trust in, and rely on the Son that we discover life in the power of His name. This good life He wants for us is Jesus Himself, and all the fulfilled promises of walking with Him should be splashing out of us and drenching the world with God's love.

Like John, I want to show you that Jesus is who He said He was: the Son of God sent to forgive our sins and make a way for us to keep company with God. I want to help you experience the reality of friendship with Jesus, to believe and keep believing. To keep believing, regardless of the multiplied craziness around us, regardless of how Jesus is going about His kingdom-building business and despite how silly, ineffective, and faulty some of His carpenters can be (all five fingers pointing back at me here).

We really can seize the good life God has for us in Jesus. It's within our reach to live fearlessly and joyfully in an anxious and angry world. John is going to show us how, and while he's at it, he's going to be very open with how often he and his friends misunderstood Jesus, failed to trust Him, and struggled to keep pace with Him. Sound familiar? They weren't perfect. They were people, just like us. But Jesus's inner circle went from quivering and questioning followers to courageous disciples whose witness rocked their world, and we can, too! It's okay if your voice is a bit shaky and there are tears on your cheeks. Jesus has all the strength you and I will ever need.

Hugs,
Shellie

How to Use This Book

L et's take a moment to get oriented. This Bible study is a little different than others you may have done—which is understandable, because I'm a little different, or so I've been told once, twice, or a hundred times. (It took years, but I've learned to be okay with that and trust God has purpose in it.)

Seizing the Good Life has twenty-one chapters, corresponding to the chapters of John's gospel. The chapters have three segments: Dear John, Dear Reader, and Dear Jesus. Peek over my shoulder in the Dear John letters as I imagine what it'd be like to discuss the gospel with the apostle who authored it. (Please know this is not intended to be a séance. God's Word opposes any such thing, and so do I.) My hope is for us to use our God-given imaginations to understand what it was like when Jesus broke into John's world so we might better recognize Him in ours. He is as present here as He was there.

We'll explore the Scriptures in the Dear Reader sections. I'll offer commentary and share my takeaways from John's gospel on how to live fearlessly and joyfully in our post-Christian world, but the margins are all yours to scribble in as you wish. I encourage you to engage with the material! Pen your own questions and listen for the Lord to answer. Note observations you may have or use a highlighter to mark thoughts you want to revisit alone or with your study group.

In the Dear Jesus sections, we'll pray about the truths we've taken from that chapter and ask Father God to establish them in our hearts. Questions and additional Scripture references follow for private use or study group aids. That said, this Bible teacher would love nothing more than hearing that the margins of your books are so heavy with discussion starters you can't even get to mine!

And now a closing thought for group leaders: I suggest approaching *Seizing the Good Life* three chapters at a time and then coming together for discussion. For example, you might have an introductory meeting to distribute books and direct your group to read the first three chapters and answer the accompanying questions. The following week, your group would meet to unpack those nine questions. This is where members could bring up notes they've penned in the margins. With twenty-one chapters in the book, such a framework would result in a seven-week study, not counting that pre-party. (Well, I don't suppose you have to make the introductory meeting a pre-party. That could just be your party-looking-for-a-place-to-happen friend speaking.) Do move slower if necessary. The point should never be how much material we can get through but how much truth the Spirit of God gets through to us!

In short, I'm inviting you to settle in and live with John's gospel, because I'm forever changed by the time I've spent in its pages, and I believe you will be, too! Let's do this.

CHAPTER ONE

Realize You Are Purposed and Equipped for These Days

D ear John,

I'm super excited about finally sitting down to write you, and fairly nervous. I considered opening with my habitual greeting, "I hope this finds you well." That's crazy, right? What with you being in Heaven! Would that have amused you? Maybe you and Jesus would've laughed together. I can't wait to hear Jesus laugh out loud! But forgive the strange opening. I'll start over with a proper introduction.

Hello John, my name is Shellie. I'm good with just using first names if you are. It feels silly to introduce myself to someone I've spent so much time with, though I suppose the familiarity is one-sided. You might not know I've been buried in your gospel for months now. Or do you? Perhaps you've seen me poring over your words and scribbling in all the margins. If so, did you roll your eyes at my never-ending questions? Do people roll their eyes in Heaven? I have a lot more questions where those came from, John.

I live in a small American town in the twenty-first century, miles and oceans from the land you called home. Generations have come and gone, governments and empires, too. And daily life? Where do I start? It's changed in ways you'd have to see to believe. If you were here, I could pick up my smartphone and call you from one side of the world—and if you answered from the other side, we could literally see each other while we talked! But you don't know what a smartphone is, do you? More on what we call "developments" later.

The thing is, John—and this is where I want to park—people today don't seem all that different than those you describe in your time. I see us in all your stories. For example, it feels like we live in an endless power struggle, with everyone vying for influence and position. You know the type—religious leaders demanding allegiance to their dogmas, more concerned about building their platforms and protecting their brands than meeting the needs of their tribes. That's right. We've got our own versions of Pharisees and Sadducees. We have Calvinists, Armenians, complementarians, egalitarians, conservatives, progressives, and, well, I'll stop there. Suffice it to say, it feels like we have more dividing us than uniting us. Sound familiar? And that's just the state of our religious leaders. More on the individual church members shortly. Right now, you need to brace yourself. The view is far darker in the unbelieving world around us.

While much of the Church fights among themselves as to who does Christianity best, our culture has quit pretending to care whether God even exists. They call it post-Christianity, meaning the world is no longer restrained by Christian ideas. Christians once wielded considerable influence in society. Not anymore. The Church has become increasingly irrelevant. Our faith is amusing to some, puzzling to others, and threatening to many. I hope you're still reading. I probably sound like Debbie Downer, but I'm not! I consider myself an informed optimist. I'm just attempting to give you the lay of the land. Bear with me a little longer.

In addition to the power struggle at the top, we also live in a perpetual popularity contest. It's influence-peddling on steroids. Everyone wants influence, and people go to extreme lengths to get it. (*Extreme*, John. You don't want me to elaborate.) Years ago, we had a popular saying: "Image is everything!" That pretty much defines us, John. And by *us*, I include a lot of believers as well as skeptics.

The goal for many is to be seen, to track how many times they're seen, and compare it with how many times other people are seen. I kid you not. People curate their images and promote themselves to other people who are too busy curating and promoting their own images to see anyone else's, which leaves everyone trying even harder to get attention (or as we prefer to say, "to make a difference"). I wish I could see your face. I picture you frowning. It's easy to see why people who aren't following Jesus promote themselves, but I imagine you're trying to understand how believers could be part of such an ugly cycle. That's a big question. Here's my two cents.

Remember when I said God is irrelevant in our culture? A similar disconnect can be found in the Church. The average believer is unwilling to yield to God's will if it conflicts with his wants. I don't believe that's a conscious decision. I think it happens for a host of reasons I hope to discuss with you in other letters. For now,

I'll state the obvious: I'm convinced we wouldn't be marketing who we are if we were taken by the glorious reality of who Jesus is!

Did I hear an amen, John? I thought I might. I adore the way you spent your entire gospel marveling over the mystery of God becoming man. You never did get over it, did you? I don't want to, either! It's the addictive power of popularity and influence that makes what John the Baptist did in your day all the more remarkable, but I'll need to pause for a confession and a fun fact.

Back when I first fell in love with your gospel, I had to train myself to remember that you, John the Disciple writing it, were not the John the Baptist described in it. That's the confession. Here's the fun fact. As a little girl growing up at Melbourne Baptist Church, I thought we were one up on all the other denominations, what with John being a Baptist and all. It'd be some time before I realized how faulty my reasoning was and even longer before I was comfortable admitting it.

But about that wild man, John the Baptist. What a show-stopping, crowd-gathering, people-magnet he turned out to be! That level of charisma makes his response to the ensuing fanfare incredibly intriguing. At the height of his popularity, when he had the crowds' attention and was gaining followers, The Baptist voluntarily deplatformed himself to point the world to Jesus.

Whoa. That makes me want to know Jesus as intimately as the two of you did, so that I, too, might live so taken with Him that nothing this world offers and no threat it makes could ever hijack my worship. It's why I've spent so much time in your gospel, John. Your words make me believe I can.

Hugs,
Shellie

Dear Reader,

I have experience in trying to capture an audience's attention and hold it long enough to get to my message. It's why I open meetings and Bible studies with storytelling and confessions of my zanier-than-I-should-be escapades. The stories serve as appetizers while the crowd gives me the once-over, drawing conclusions about whether they should care about anything I'm there to say based on how I look and what I'm wearing. (Isn't it funny that they think I don't notice?) I believe the self-effacing humor is disarming and helps prepare my listeners for the Word.

John's communication style is the polar opposite. The man opens at full speed, and he's laser-focused on his main subject as he regales us with one passionate description of Jesus after another. Our first passage is lengthy and so worthy of our attention. Let's stay in it and consider the sheer majesty of this otherworldly being John attempts to define in human terms.

> [1] In the beginning was the Word, and the Word was with God, and the Word was God. [2] He was in the beginning with God. [3] All things came into being through Him, and apart from Him not even one thing came into being that has come into being. [4] In Him was life, and the life was the Light of mankind. [5] And the Light shines in the darkness, and the darkness did not grasp it. [6] A man came, one sent from God, and his name was John. [7] He came as a witness, to testify about the Light, so that all might believe through him. [8] He was not the Light, but he came to testify about the Light. [9] This was the true Light that, coming into the world, enlightens every person. [10] He was

in the world, and the world came into being through Him, and yet the world did not know Him. [11] He came to His own, and His own people did not accept Him. [12] But as many as received Him, to them He gave the right to become children of God, to those who believe in His name, [13] who were born, not of blood, nor of the will of the flesh, nor of the will of a man, but of God.

[14] And the Word became flesh, and dwelt among us; and we saw His glory, glory as of the only Son from the Father, full of grace and truth. [15] John testified about Him and called out, saying, "This was He of whom I said, 'He who is coming after me has proved to be my superior, because He existed before me.'" [16] For of His fullness we have all received, and grace upon grace. [17] For the Law was given through Moses; grace and truth were realized through Jesus Christ. [18] No one has seen God at any time; God the only Son, who is in the arms of the Father, He has explained Him.

Whew! John is a frenzied artist adding breathless strokes until a portrait like no other stands before us. Only then does he catch his breath and invite us into the rest of his gospel. And yet, we'll soon see that John never stops trying to wrap words around the mystery of God's Son walking among mankind.

John the Writer barely concludes his enthusiastic effort to help us comprehend that God Himself has appeared on earth in the image of His Son before he practically strips gears to introduce John the Baptist, a man who has arrived preaching a similar message, with a show-stopping twist. The Baptist announces that this

Magnificent Being whom the Writer has been describing is God's promised Messiah, and He's already on the scene. But then he takes it a step further. The Baptist proclaims that this much-anticipated Messiah is also God's chosen Lamb. A lamb, you say?! Hit the brakes!

John's audience would've immediately associated lambs with bloody sacrifices and sin offerings. What a mysterious dichotomy. This magnificent Being has come to die as God's Sacrificial Lamb? Remember the humility we noted in the Baptist? Jesus models humility that's infinitely more startling. He's the Light of the World, stepping down to serve as the Lamb who dies for it. But I'm getting ahead of myself. Let's pace this out.

The other gospels tell us John the Baptist showed up wearing hairy clothes and snacking on bugs and honey (Matthew 3:4; Mark 1:6). Those fashion choices and dietary details don't warrant a mention by our gospel writer. Keeping to his theme—that the Creator has come to live with the created—John the Writer skips to The Baptist's insistence that he is merely the Messiah's messenger. It's the Lamb who deserves top billing.

Interestingly, when John the Baptist first began proclaiming that Christ was on the scene, he stopped shy of pointing him out in the crowd because at that juncture, John couldn't identify Him. All he knew was that Messiah had come. But that all changed when Cousin Jesus got in John's baptism line!

I haven't baptized anyone in years, but as a kid, I had a flourishing ministry in this doctrinal area. Sisters, cousins, friends, anyone willing to play church with me in that small, heavily chlorinated community pool in Tallulah, Louisiana, was dunked in the name of "the Father, the Son, and the Holy Ghost." I may have even baptized candidates who weren't feeling the call but ventured too close to my baptismal waters. This led to some drama, but nothing like what happened that day in Bethany! No one had seen anything like it before. No one has seen anything like it since.

> [29] The next day he saw Jesus coming to him, and said, "Behold, the Lamb of God who takes away the sin of the world! [30] This is He on behalf of whom I said, 'After me is coming a Man who has proved to be my superior, because He existed before me.' [31] And I did not recognize Him, but so that He would be revealed to Israel, I came baptizing in water." [32] And John testified, saying, "I have seen the Spirit descending as a dove out of heaven, and He remained upon Him. [33] And I did not recognize Him, but He who sent me to baptize in water said to me, 'He upon whom you see the Spirit descending and remaining upon Him, this is the One who baptizes in the Holy Spirit.' [34] And I myself have seen and have testified that this is the Son of God."

We're not told how much time Jesus and John the Baptist had spent together before this, but it was enough for Jesus to earn His cousin's respect. We know this because Matthew tells us The Baptist was initially hesitant about baptizing Jesus, insisting it should be vice versa. John only relented when Jesus insisted (Matthew 3:14), and he only recognized Jesus as the Messiah once he baptized Him because of God's previously established supernatural sign. In an eternity-driven revelation too consequential to be left to the faculties of man, the Spirit descended upon Jesus like a dove, and the Father's voice was heard from Heaven proclaiming, *"You are my beloved Son, in You I am well pleased"* (Luke 3:22).

The Spirit descending like a dove is more than poetic detail. Scriptures often use a dove to depict God's Spirit. If we connect dove imagery from Genesis with the New Testament words of Jesus, we can savor the hope of this supernaturally charged moment at the river's edge.

Genesis 1:1–2 reads,

> In the beginning God created the heavens and the earth.
> And the earth was a formless and desolate emptiness,
> and darkness was over the surface of the deep, and the
> Spirit of God was hovering over the surface of the waters.

We're told that God's Spirit was hovering. The NET Bible has this to say about the Hebrew verb that's translated here as "hovering." It means: "'to brood over; to incubate.' How much of that sense might be attached here is hard to say, but the verb does depict the presence of the Spirit of God moving about mysteriously over the waters, presumably preparing for the acts of creation to follow."

The Gospel good news is that God's Spirit does more than hover over us today when our lives feel dark, formless, and void. Because of the finished work of the Cross, the Spirit of God literally indwells believers to bring about His purposes! Where life feels meaningless, He is present to form purpose. Where life feels empty, He is willing to fill. We're headed back to the New Testament to see this promise in Jesus's own words, but first, let's grab one more reference to the dove from Genesis 8.

We'll be jumping into the familiar story of the great Flood. The rains have stopped, and Noah is repeatedly releasing a dove from a window in the ark to check for dry land.

> [9] But the dove found no resting place for the sole of its foot, so it returned to him in the ark, for the water was on the surface of all the earth. Then he put out his hand and took it, and brought it into the ark to himself. [10] So he waited another seven days longer; and again he sent out the dove from the ark. [11] And the dove came to him in the evening, and behold, in its beak was a fresh olive leaf. So, Noah knew that the water was low on the earth. [12] Then he waited another seven days longer, and sent out the dove; but it did not return to him again.

When Noah realized the dove wasn't returning, he and his family left the ark along with the animals, and life on earth began again. It was a fresh start, but it wasn't Eden. That ship had sailed. (Sorry. It was too easy.) The storyteller in me imagines that dove circling the heavens throughout the ages, waiting for God's signal to alight again—this time on the Son of Man who would restore the relationship between God and His creation that was severed in the garden. It's a cool picture, but that's all it is—imagery. Let's not make doctrines out of our imagination when the Word is our authority, and it holds ample encouragement to quiet our twenty-first-century hearts. I'll show you.

In John 1:32, The Writer describes God's Holy Spirit coming in the form of a dove to rest on Jesus and remain on Him. We tend to think, "That's great...for Jesus." But it's much more than that. It's our present-tense promise.

Having reconciled us to God and returned to heaven, Jesus sent that very same Spirit to remain with us. Nourish yourself in this pledge from His own mouth.

> But I tell you the truth: it is to your advantage that I am leaving; for if I do not leave, the Helper will not come to you; but if I go, I will send Him to you. (John 16:7)

Had Jesus remained in the flesh, He wouldn't have been able to be with each of us at all times. But He did return to the Father, and His Spirit has come to live in and remain with all who believe. Seize that encouragement, friend. While the world is growing increasingly impatient with Jesus-followers, if not openly hostile, we can plant our shaky selves on the same wonderful truth the disciples enjoyed. The Spirit of God is with us, and we're alive on Planet Earth in these challenging days by divine purpose, not random assignment.

> And He made from one man every nation of mankind to live on all the face of the earth, having determined their appointed times and the boundaries of their habitation. (Acts 17:26)

You and I were purposed to live in these days, and we've been given the opportunity to do so indwelt by the power and presence of Almighty God. When we rush through our lives without seeking

Him, we live at the mercy of stress-inducing news that's always building and breaking. But, praise God, the opposite is also true! If we live asking Jesus to help us trust Him and make Him our everything, He'll do that and more. He'll make Himself the cornerstone of our lives, and then He'll reach through us to the world around us. This is our inheritance. We can access the wisdom and power of God while we're still here on Earth, and our souls can know peace where the world says there is none. How do we experience such a supernatural heritage? We'll explore that in the pages ahead. Pray with me?

Dear Jesus,

Help us grasp the supernatural wonder of who You are and the miracle of Your coming from beyond our world to show us the way home. You not only made a way for us to follow You there; You opened a way for us to live with You here. Give us fresh eyes to comprehend this mystery and a hunger to experience its reality. And would You start with me? I can be optimistic one minute and worried the next. When I get preoccupied with curating the best life I can for me and mine, and my eyes fall to this world as if this life is all there is, the rising darkness of our time slams into me, making me feel helpless and anxious over the future my kids and grandkids are inheriting.

But You are the Eternal Word, giving life to everything, bringing light to everyone, and perfectly demonstrating God's unfailing love and faithfulness for His creation. Help me look to You before I look around me so I can walk in Your light and reflect Your light to those around me. When my eyes are on You, I feel promise and purpose instead of fear and anxiety. As we watch some people passively denying Your existence and others actively working to oust You from society, help us remember no one and nothing can extinguish Your light. Those who fight against You will be forever separated from You. Let this realization move us to Spirit-led compassion and intercession for their souls. Help us live encouraging others to follow You, and keep us from becoming an obstacle to them by falling into the trap of influence-peddling. We confess that, left to ourselves, we can even make our pursuit of You about us. Deliver us from this evil.

Thank You for being the stairway connecting Heaven and Earth, allowing us to experience the stabilizing joy of living with You in our turbulent world. Forgive us for not making more use of this divine access we've been granted, for only in Your presence can we find the courage to live bold lives that hold out Your glorious invitation to those around us. Teach us how to be supernatural stair climbers. In Your blessed name we pray, Jesus. Amen.

For Discussion

1. Read Isaiah 40:3 and Malachi 3:1. John the Baptist knew he was called to prepare the way for God's promised Son, but he arrived preaching about the Messiah being present in their world without actually knowing His identity. In what ways could that have been challenging for John?

2. Read 2 Corinthians 7:10 and Acts 11:18. John preached a water baptism signifying repentance, which was a turning away from sin. The Jewish community was

familiar with water baptism for converts who turned to Judaism from other religions but not for those born Jews. Explore what it would have meant for a Jew to accept John's message that being born a Jew wasn't enough. What might it have cost them to accept that truth? Do you feel like your faith in Christ is costing you? Why or why not?

3. Read John 1:43–51 and Genesis 28:10–17. Nathanael acknowledged Jesus as the Son of God because Jesus had seen him under the fig tree. We don't always feel seen by God, do we? Jesus told Nathaniel there was something better ahead than being seen by God and referenced the story of Jacob's Ladder. In your own words, what greater reality do you think Jesus was referring to in verse 51?

CHAPTER TWO

Trust Jesus to Strengthen Your Faith and Transform Your Heart

Dear John,

I just reread my first letter to you. Confession? It was embarrassing to see how I went on and on about our self-promoting, self-obsessed culture, and how I put it right down here in black and white so God and everybody could read it. File this under ironic: I was thinking I didn't exactly put my best foot forward when something occurred to me. I was concerned my telling you about our preoccupation with what other people think of us would leave you with a poor impression of me! Again, it's okay if you're laughing. I am. We have a saying, "Old habits die hard." The longer I aim to live this crucified life with Jesus, the more aware I am that my old nature has to be crucified daily! But that's a conversation I look forward to having with the Apostle Paul. Warn him. I mean, give him my best. (Come on, John. You know that was funny!)

Seems to me your story of the wedding in Cana has plenty of this pride-and-pretense pit. And, once more, the people of your day act so much like us, it's startling. That whole, "They have no more wine" moment when Mary confronts Jesus with the supply problem has an anxiousness about it that suggests the party was about to be over, along with the public standing of those who sent out the invites. You didn't explain why Mary was so invested in the festivities, but I've read where some scholars believe she was related to the hosts. If that's the case, I understand. Several years ago, my son and my daughter (fruit of my womb who claim to love me) married their respective sweethearts in the very same summer, within weeks of each other. I have vivid memories of that season's pressure! We could've used a miracle or two ourselves.

But back to the Cana party. You wrote how the wine ran out during the festivities. I'm guessing here, but since Jesus had yet to perform a miracle, it's hard to imagine any of y'all were anticipating him to up and save the day. Except for Mary. Right? *Somehow*, Mary was expecting Jesus to do *something*.

I bet she was beaming from ear to ear when Jesus produced that wine. But what about you and the other disciples? You said neither the host nor the crowd were informed of where the good wine came from, only the servants. It seems Jesus performed His first miracle for you guys. What's interesting is how you recorded that it caused all of you to believe in Him. I found that initially perplexing. I mean, you were His disciples! I thought you already believed.

However, the longer I sat with your words, the more I began to understand. You know what I decided? I think you believed before, but your faith got a booster shot when Jesus turned that water to wine! Thank you for your openness, John. Knowing Jesus acted to reinforce the faith of those of you who were following Him then encourages me to trust that He is doing the same thing for us now! Circumstances are always challenging our faith. It helps to know Jesus is orchestrating opportunities to strengthen it.

I need to tell you a story. I was in a hotel room one Saturday morning not long ago preparing to speak to a group of Jesus-loving women. We had already met the night before. God had moved among us, and it had been good. Very good. And yet, that next morning, the health issues of a loved one were weighing on me. As I asked God to give her relief from what seemed like never-ending trauma, I became aware that my desire for her restoration was struggling with my unbelief that anything would change. That realization flooded me with guilt. How could I doubt the God I love when He has been faithful to me time and again? Worse, how could I doubt Him and then stand before His people? And why did He even allow it?

My prayer took a new direction as I began to ask the Lord to forgive my unbelief. I remember telling Him, "You're so good. You deserve so much more. You deserve obedience that never hesitates. You deserve faithfulness that never wavers. You deserve belief that never doubts...and you got me." The Lord doesn't speak to me audibly, but over time, His Voice has become increasingly familiar. I was knee-deep in that litany of what I knew He deserved when everything in me felt Him say, "And I got it. I got all that sinless perfection in Jesus, and you get to stand in it."

Moments like that stick with a person, don't they, John? We can't explain why He is so long-suffering with us, but when we choose to believe it, we get to experience His faithful Presence.

My confession and God's response reminds me of something you wrote towards the end of this chapter, "Many believed in His name as they observed His signs which He was doing. But Jesus, on His part, was not entrusting Himself to them... for He Himself knew what was in mankind" (John 2:23–25). I get it. Jesus understood the fickle nature of men's hearts, but He wasn't depressed or shaken by it, for His confidence and security rested in the good heart of His Father. Wow. #lifegoals (That's called a hashtag, John. I'll explain later.)

Hugs,
Shellie

Dear Reader,

I had some fun little tea towels made for my website that I also make available on my product table when I'm speaking at women's events. The towels sport a tongue-in-cheek query, "Y'all get enough to eat?" The question is a tribute to the women in my family, and it's followed with a small print definition, "Southern saying often used by women serving a feast to question those consuming it."

My tea towels elicit many a chuckle from women who have either been quizzed by that line or used it to question others. Some of us Southerners have migrated to a healthier diet over the years and some of us can still turn a vegetable into a dessert, but one thing continues to unite us: we like to feed people. No self-respecting

Southern hostess can abide the thought of running out of food before everyone is topped off and begging for mercy. By all accounts, the culture of Mary's day had a similar attitude about the wine served at weddings. There's a heap of good news waiting for us in the story of Jesus's first recorded miracle, and it goes much deeper than helping the party planners avoid a social failure.

> [1] On the third day there was a wedding in Cana of Galilee, and the mother of Jesus was there; [2] and both Jesus and His disciples were invited to the wedding. [3] When the wine ran out, the mother of Jesus said to Him, "They have no wine." [4] And Jesus said to her, "What business do you have with Me, woman? My hour has not yet come." [5] His mother said to the servants, "Whatever He tells you, do it." [6] Now there were six stone waterpots standing there for the Jewish custom of purification, containing [twenty or thirty gallons] each. [7] Jesus said to them, "Fill the waterpots with water." So they filled them up to the brim. [8] And He said to them, "Draw some out now and take it to the headwaiter." And they took it to him. [9] Now when the headwaiter tasted the water which had become wine, and did not know where it came from (but the servants who had drawn the water knew), the headwaiter called the groom, [10] and said to him, "Every man serves the good wine first, and when the guests are drunk, then he serves the poorer wine; but you have kept the good wine until now." [11] This beginning of His signs Jesus did in Cana of Galilee, and revealed His glory, and His disciples believed in Him. (John 2)

Historians tell us wedding festivities in Jesus's day often lasted an entire week, and the host was expected to serve food and drink for the duration. (Let us pause to give thanks for changing times.) That custom suggests this gathering was anything but a spontaneous shindig with little thought to how much wine would be enough. This party would've been carefully planned, with the to-do list checked and rechecked, and still the unthinkable happened. I can relate.

Heads up: This could be where my teetotaling friends and my all-things-in-moderation friends debate the consumption of wine. Let's not. Instead, join me in savoring the graciousness of Jesus. He didn't chastise the host for not planning well enough, and He didn't opine on whether the guests had already enjoyed enough. Instead, Jesus brought His more-than-enough Self to the moment and helped the host avoid embarrassment while simultaneously elevating the man to a position of honor.

Throughout God's Word, wine symbolizes joy and vitality, blessing and prosperity, such that makes glad man's heart. Jesus is God's good wine, promised and given at the end of the age. He is the Joy of our salvation, and He is more than enough. If only we didn't look like the wedding guests in this story who drank up and partied on, clueless to the Presence of their benefactor.

Jesus's first miracle was one of transformation. Let's not miss that. It's a beautiful illustration of what Jesus does for believers. He not only cancels our shame and lifts us up, but much as the new wine exceeded the expectations of the steward in this story, Jesus stands ready to exceed our expectations of what it means to know Him. To seize the overflowing life of Christ in us, we'll have to quit settling for the temporary fixes around us and live in His Presence and in His Word until His company changes our want-tos—until our cravings for the things around us pale in light of our desire for more of Him.

This is the transformative miracle that mirrors the water becoming wine, the one Jesus stands ready to do in all who believe. By faith, we experience a new birth that is supernatural and initially unseen, but the outworking of this inside job only becomes evident as we live with Him. It's in training our eyes on Jesus that we become what we haven't been.

A few years back, I fell in love with 2 Corinthians 3:18. It holds out that promise with these words:

> And we all, with unveiled face, beholding the glory of
> the Lord, are being transformed into the same image
> from one degree of glory to another. For this comes from
> the Lord who is the Spirit. (ESV)

Jesus does not take over our wills at our rebirth. We retain the right to choose whether we will continue to believe and behold Him. The choice we make can leave us living like Christian atheists or propel us forward and transform us by increments. But know this: We won't go back again and again to draw on the steady infusion of joy and peace Jesus offers until we understand that He isn't poised to rap our foreheads when we feel more like Doubting Thomas than Apostle Paul. On the contrary, Jesus is present to reveal His glory to us and strengthen our faith to keep believing. We can see that good news in verse 11,

> This beginning of His signs Jesus did in Cana of
> Galilee, and revealed His glory; and His disciples
> believed in Him.

Remember, Jesus stayed out of the limelight during the wine-making wonder of this initial sign. That means the crowds didn't see the glory He chose to reveal. His disciples did. And the result, according to Scripture, is that they believed.

The disciples, who already believed, believed again. If you're anxious and weary from wondering if the whole world has gone crazy and God has washed His hands of our twenty-first-century selves, here lies proof that it's okay to need a booster shot to keep believing. What's more, Jesus is here for it! As surely as He revealed His glory through the miracle in Cana, Jesus lives to reveal Himself to you and to me. He comes to us in our emptiness and in our lack to show us that He is more than enough.

This won't be the last time we'll get to see the guys' faith growing as they stumble after Messiah. Let we who stumble after Jesus today live watching and waiting for His next revelation of Himself to us!

Sometimes, when I'm full of praise and gratitude and feeling woefully inept at expressing it, I'm reassured to remember the Lord knows every thought of my heart. There are other times when it can be frightening to be so thoroughly known by Him. Anybody? Hold tightly to this truth with me. Jesus doesn't ask us to trust in our ability to love Him or our capacity to believe and follow Him. He asks us to trust in how He loves us and in His finished work of grace. That's good news to this writer. Let's pray.

Dear Jesus,

Mary asked you for help and then she told the servants to do whatever You told them to do. That challenges me. I tend to pray about my problems and tell You how to fix them in the same breath. Forgive me. Help me to pray, trust You to respond, and stand ready to act on Your instruction.

Jesus, we believe your Father and ours sent us prophets and saints to testify to Your coming, but You alone are the Good Wine that was saved for the appointed time. Discovering You as our true joy strengthens us to live in this world. Sadly, we confess that we can taste how good You are and still be prone to filling ourselves with the lesser wines of this earth. Forgive us, and remind us to drink long and often at the well You have opened within us, the fount of living water that flows from Father God's throne. Alert us when we're reaching for temporary fixes to satisfy the cravings of our soul that You alone can fill. We honor You as God's greatest gift, and we acknowledge that You are more than enough. Unite our hearts to build our lives on this truth. You are better-than, and everything else is lesser-than.

Thank You, Jesus, for showing us in the Word that You intentionally encouraged the faith of Your disciples. We want to keep believing, too. We own our need to abide in You and listen to You to do it! Help us remember the message You inspired Paul to write that tells us faith comes by hearing, and hearing by the Word of God. Stir our hunger for Your words, that the faith that saved us might increase in us as we nourish ourselves in Your life-giving, faith-building words. In Your precious name we pray, and in your completed work we rest. Amen.

For Discussion

. . . .

1. Read Psalm 104:15, Proverbs 3:10, Nehemiah 8:10–12, and 1 Corinthians 11:23–26. Scripture connects wine with joy and overflowing blessing but forbids drinking to excess (Ephesians 5:18). Compare the symbolism of wine representing Christ's blood with the abundance of wine He made at the wedding. What might be the result Jesus expects us to experience by keeping the Lord's Supper and remembering the shedding of His blood? Does the Bible set limits on that expectation? Do we? Be prepared to explain your answer.

2. Read Jeremiah 33:8, Titus 2:14, and 1 Corinthians 6:19–20. What similarity do you see between Jesus's first work in the earthly temple and His first work in our lives? Verse 17 of John 2 speaks of Jesus's passion for the temple. Discuss whether you believe Scripture is talking about the physical temple in Jerusalem or the earthly ones we inhabit.

3. Read Romans 10:17, 1 Thessalonians 2:13, and Galatians 3:1–3. In these verses, we can find instructions on how we can continue to believe and keep believing so that we might mature in the faith. We can also find an admonishment about the grown plan that fails every time. Identify the two plans and discuss the differences.

CHAPTER THREE

Look Away from Yourself and Live

D ear John,
   I don't know why you're the only gospel writer who wrote
of Nicodemus, but thank you for introducing us to him. That first
nighttime visit with Jesus is quite the dramatic read, and your
record of it produced what has become one of the most beloved
Jesus quotes of all time. *"For God so loved the world that He gave
His one and only Son, that whoever believes in Him shall not
perish but have eternal life"* (NIV). It's been called the most famous
verse in the Bible. That's a good thing, right, John? It's got it all.
God so loved us that He gave His Son to cross the divide our sin
created and bring us home, forever.

By the way, would it surprise you to hear that Nicodemus has
taken a lot of flak through the years for coming to Jesus under the
cover of darkness? I've heard sermons making him out to be the

poster boy for what it looks like to allow the fear of men to keep us from following Jesus. I suppose that could've been your intention in the way you introduced him, but that's not what I get after reading your full gospel. I wonder if perhaps you wanted us to see Nicodemus progress from furtive seeker to open follower. Besides, I dare say none of us would fare well if we were frozen in a moment when we have more fear than faith and that scene was billed as our life story.

It's why I'm thankful to have your account of Nicodemus's full story, beginning with this first meeting with Jesus. I love the understanding side of Jesus it reveals. I find it amazing that He didn't shame the Pharisee for coming to him secretly, but I'm tremendously encouraged by what happened next. As they begin to converse, I see Jesus showing remarkable patience with Nicodemus for being slow to understand the life He was calling him to embrace. That last line has my name all over it.

Instead, Jesus simply engages with Nicodemus without taking offense at his questions. This is the Jesus I've come to know and the One who becomes dearer still the longer I follow Him. He is so longsuffering with my remedial self! We silly humans are prone to thinking we have to figure out how it all works so we can walk with Him. We have it backwards, don't we? Jesus invites us to walk with Him so He can show us how it all works. He nourishes our interest in Him and builds our faith on the journey. It's what He did for you and your friends, and He's still doing it for us today. What a Savior!

But about those rule-keeping, ritual-loving people of your day. Let's just say I can relate to them, though it took a long time for me to see how much we had in common. At first, I thought they were silly, clinging to all their old ways of serving God with sacrifices and burnt offerings when Jesus was standing right there in front of them. I couldn't figure out what it was about obsessively obeying the law that they found so appealing. My rituals, on the other hand? I saw them as sincere, honest efforts to connect with Jesus. Finding out they were actually keeping me from knowing Him the way I longed to know Him was a major turning point in my life.

Of course, I wouldn't have called the things I was doing rituals, and I would've totally bristled had anyone else suggested it, but I was dedicated to checking off the boxes because it made me feel like I was welcome with Him. Same thing, right? I thought so.

Honestly, I think it's hard for all of us to swim in the deep end of grace consistently. It takes faith to hold onto the truth that we're always warmly welcome and fully accepted by God through Jesus. At least that's been my experience! I love celebrating His amazing grace that invites me to join Him in what He is doing around me, instead of working to earn the acceptance I've already been given. The problem comes in when the scary stuff hits and the things I can see threaten to shake my trust and rest in the One I can't. That's when I'm prone to revisiting that old mentality and feeling like my fears are failure, my faith is a disappointment, and I can't expect God to come through for me because I've fallen down on Him. Ugh. We both know that kind of thinking only complicates anxiety and deters us from calling out for divine reinforcement! But, hey, I'm getting there. I'm less susceptible to that pit than I've ever been, and I credit your gospel with teaching me to avoid it. Thank you. Until next time, John.

Hugs,
Shellie

Dear Reader,

The third chapter of John opens with a leader of the Jews named Nicodemus admitting to Jesus that he and his peers knew He was a teacher sent from God because of the miracles He'd been performing. This would've been breaking news for the larger community, but Nicodemus offered it under cover of darkness in a "just between us" type of meeting. Jesus accepted that implied coronation without comment and raised the stakes with an equally startling response. Read the first part of their exchange, then meet me below.

[1] Now there was a man of the Pharisees, named Nicodemus, a ruler of the Jews; [2] this man came to Jesus at night and said to Him, "Rabbi, we know that You have come from God as a teacher; for no one can do these signs that You do unless God is with him." [3] Jesus responded and said to him, "Truly, truly, I say to you, unless someone is born again he cannot see the kingdom of God."

[4] Nicodemus said to Him, "How can a person be born when he is old? He cannot enter his mother's womb a second time and be born, can he?" [5] Jesus answered, "Truly, truly, I say to you, unless someone is born of water and the Spirit, he cannot enter the kingdom of God. [6] That which has been born of the flesh is flesh, and that which has been born of the Spirit is spirit. [7] Do not be amazed that I said to you, 'You must be born again.' [8] The wind blows where it wishes, and you hear the sound of it, but you do not know where it is coming from and where it is going; so is everyone who has been born of the Spirit."

> [9] Nicodemus responded and said to Him, "How can these things be?" [10] Jesus answered and said to him, "You are the teacher of Israel, and yet you do not understand these things?"

I've looked. I can't find a single commentary that even alludes to what I'm about to say, but I'm going to barrel ahead anyway. The thing is, I've got my suspicions about whether Nicodemus was sincerely confused when he asked if Jesus was suggesting a grown man could climb back into his mother's womb, or if there was more going on between the two of them. This is just me thinking aloud. It's not a new doctrine. We can't say authoritatively because the Bible doesn't, but it would help to explain why Jesus was so quick to chastise Nicodemus for not understanding, even after His fuller explanation. Stay with me.

As a rabbi, Nicodemus was steeped in the Jewish Torah (the first five books of what we call "The Old Testament"). It's highly likely he had the entirety memorized. And while we can't find expressly written words about a new birth in those manuscripts, they contain abundant teaching on the spiritual death (separation from God) that entered our world in the Fall of Adam and Eve, as well as ongoing illustrations of how that death spread to all mankind.

Furthermore, the Old Testament records many instances of God promising that one day, He would come and remove His people's stony hearts and give them new hearts so that He could dwell with them forever. Here's one example:

> And I will give them one heart, and a new spirit I will put within them. I will remove the heart of stone from

their flesh and give them a heart of flesh, that they may
walk in my statutes and keep my rules and obey them.
And they shall be my people, and I will be their God.
(Ezekiel 11:19–20 ESV)

I believe Jesus expected Nicodemus to understand that man's
spirit was dead on its own, and man's spirit needed God's promise
of new life. Nicodemus would've been fine had Jesus said Gentiles
needed this awakening experience to know God. But to say that
Jew and Gentile alike needed to start at the same place? This was
outrageous teaching! Acquiescing to it was scary because it went
against their religious teachings. Even worse, it threatened to make
Nicodemus and his fellow leaders—wait for it—expendable.

Nicodemus and his fellow rabbis were teaching others that righteousness came from strict adherence to the Jewish Law they were
in charge of overseeing, and their list of rules continued to grow far
beyond God's original commandments. Jesus was asking Nicodemus
to acknowledge what we all know: nobody can be that perfect.

Regardless of how we try, we can't "will ourselves right." We need
Jesus to save us, and we need Jesus to sustain us. He is more than
willing and always ready, but we must be intentional about laying
hold of the promise. Jesus is about to remind Nicodemus of another
story that will be familiar to him and underscore this necessity.

[11] Truly, truly, I say to you, we speak of what we know
and testify of what we have seen, and you people do not
accept our testimony. [12] If I told you earthly things and
you do not believe, how will you believe if I tell you
heavenly things? [13] No one has ascended into heaven,

except He who descended from heaven: the Son of Man.
¹⁴ And just as Moses lifted up the serpent in the wilderness, so must the Son of Man be lifted up, ¹⁵ so that everyone who believes will have eternal life in Him.

Nicodemus has already confessed that he and his peers knew Jesus to be from God. By using both plural and singular pronouns, Jesus states the greater reality: He is more than an emissary from God; He is One with God. He is God's promised remedy for what ails man, and He came to Earth to heal all who would look to Him and believe. Jesus was alluding to an incident in the twenty-first chapter of Numbers. I'll sum the story up while you watch to find us in it.

It's set in the wilderness. Israel is traveling from Egypt to the Promised Land when God does a weird but wonderful thing. As punishment for their sins, deadly snakes are loosed among them. The bites prove fatal unless those bitten look toward a bronze snake God instructed Moses to make and attach to the top of a pole. By looking away from the painful snakebite and toward God's answer for it, they could be healed. The people would die if they ignored the bite ("I'm not a sinner!") or self-doctored it ("I can manage my sin my way!"). It's in the context of this story that Jesus speaks of Himself being lifted up for salvation and speaks the famous words of John 3:16:

> For God so loved the world, that He gave His only Son, that whoever believes in Him should not perish but have eternal life. (ESV)

Imagine, if you will, Jesus looking at the rabbi with compassion and speaking tenderly to him, imploring him to be part of the "whoever." He is always inviting us to look away from ourselves and look to Him to live. He's inviting us to believe again, today, on top of all the other days we have believed. To believe that whatever sins are plaguing us and whatever fears are assailing us, we can't overcome them in our own virtue or strength, but we can thwart the enemy's assault and find healing by looking away from ourselves and looking to Jesus again!

Would Nicodemus decide to protect his way of life, or would he come to the Light and live? We'll find those answers later in John's writing. For now, we're lowering the curtain on that famous scene. I want us to explore one more passage from the end of John 3.

> [22] After these things Jesus and His disciples came into the land of Judea; and there He was spending time with them and baptizing. [23] Now John also was baptizing in Aenon, near Salim, because there was an abundance of water there; and people were coming and being baptized— [24] for John had not yet been thrown into prison. [25] Then a matter of dispute developed on the part of John's disciples with a Jew about purification. [26] And they came to John and said to him, "Rabbi, He who was with you beyond the Jordan, to whom you have testified—behold, He is baptizing and all the people are coming to Him." [27] John replied, "A person can receive not even one thing unless it has been given to him from heaven. [28] You yourselves are my witnesses that I said, 'I am not the Christ,' but, 'I have been sent ahead of Him.' [29] He who has the bride is the groom; but the

friend of the groom, who stands and listens to him, rejoices greatly because of the groom's voice. So this joy of mine has been made full. [30] He must increase, but I must decrease."

The disciples of John the Baptist were afraid their firebrand teacher was becoming irrelevant. That sounds loyal, but I wonder if we're hearing hints of the self-interest that motivated Nicodemus. Could it be that John's disciples secretly worried about being only as relevant as their teacher? I ask because we're susceptible to falling into a similar trap. We're prone to favoring the movements of men over the message of God, too. Do we want Jesus to be famous because we'll finally be seen as the cool kids instead of the strange Bible geeks? Or do we want Jesus to be known for His glorious, soul-saving Self? Choosing the first goal results in more emptiness; the second one, increasing joy.

The reality is that there's no end to our ability to make everything about us. It's ugly, but there it is. We can even make our pursuit of God all about us. Is that embarrassing? Yes, but we're the better for owning and exposing it. I'm willing to put my hand up and ask Jesus to alert me when I'm falling into that snare and save me from such living. I've asked Him before and I'll ask Him again, because living for human affirmation is a downward spiral, whether we're after secular recognition for worldly talents or churchy acclaim for our Jesus talk. Ouch. John the Baptist knew the secret of the fulfillment we're chasing. He realized the back seat was the best seat, and the way to enjoy the ride was to make more of Jesus, less of John. Let's pray.

Dear Jesus,

We've just discussed what You already know. We can make loving You about us. Forgive us for so often looking to man for validation and approval. Wean us from this temptation. Help us hunger for You instead. We ask You to alert us when our desire to be relevant in the eyes of our circles or the online world are obscuring our desire for those around us to know You. We don't want to be prisoners to the world's approval or fearful of the world's rejection. We acknowledge that fullness of joy can't and won't be found in our social causes or our ministries. We don't want to be committed to any movement or doctrine of man over the saving message of God. Overshadow us, Jesus! Help us hide beneath Your wings.

We confess that You alone are our joy. We want to live in Your Light and live for Your glory, and we acknowledge that we can't serve You wholeheartedly apart from Your ever-present help. As we pursue You, may we live ever needy of You, always resorting to You for the infinite resources that You have made readily available to us through the Cross.

Help us hold onto the lesson You gave Nicodemus. We want to look away from our sin and keep our eyes fixed on You. We believe You are eternal life, and in looking to You, we can experience abundant life. There is no duty we can check off that merits Your Presence. Alert us when we are putting our confidence in anyone or anything other than Your atoning blood.

You are the reality of God. You came to reconcile us to the Father, that we may abide together throughout eternity, beginning now. Thank You! Help us to believe and keep believing in Your

*love for us, shown on the Cross and witnessed in our hearts. In
Your holy name we pray. Amen.*

For Discussion

1. Read Joel 2:28, Isaiah 32:15, and Isaiah 44:3. These
   verses speak of God's Spirit being poured out like
   water. Do you think this is what Jesus meant by being
   born of water, or is this referring to a different type
   of outpouring? Please explain your answer.

2. Read John 3:11–18. Count the number of times you
   find a form of the word "believe." Why do you think
   Jesus might have used this word so repetitively with
   Nicodemus?

3. Read Numbers 21:1–9. What were the Israelites complaining about when God sent the poisonous snakes
   among them? In your own words, can you explain
   why this would have been so obnoxious to God? Now
   read 1 Corinthians 10:9. This verse speaks of "testing
   the Lord." What do you think that means? Take a
   moment to record a prayer, asking the Lord to keep
   you from this trap.

CHAPTER FOUR

Guzzle Grace and Give It Away

D ear John,
 Do you like to sing? I ask because I'm ridiculously curious
by nature and you never said anything about music in your gospel,
although I understand music was a large part of your culture.
Matthew and Mark recorded how all of you sang a hymn together
after the Lord's Supper. That must've been special. I love the idea
of Jesus singing almost as much as I enjoy the idea of Him laughing.
So, what gives? Why no mention of that music? Is it because you
don't sing so well? I would understand that. I can't carry a tune
with two hands, but I'm convinced Jesus enjoys my joyful noise.

 Worship is my happy place. I'm fond of all kinds, both the old
hymns of my childhood and the contemporary praise music of our
day. Since it's just us talking, I'll tell you something else I enjoy. I have
this habit of taking lyrics from a secular song and tweaking them

here and there until they're fit for worship. It feels…redemptive, if that makes sense.

For instance, you know the woman you wrote of in Chapter 4? We call her the Samaritan woman here in the Church Age. Her story reminds me of a country song my friends and I sang years ago while we were out line dancing. (Line dancing? Think synchronized dance moves and big fun.) The opening words of the song I'm thinking of sound like something the Samaritan woman could've written, and the close—well, the Samaritan woman and I could both sing those to Jesus. I can't print all the lyrics here because we have these things called copyright laws, but here's a sample of the opening. The singer admits to spending a lifetime searching before confessing that he was "lookin' for love in all the wrong places."

Sounds like the Samaritan woman, doesn't it, John? And just like in her story, the lyrics speak of finally being found by someone who is everything she'd hoped for and the living embodiment of the dream. That old country tune is talking about a mortal man finding a mortal woman, but I love singing it to the God Man. The ending recounts my own story and captures my song. Jesus! He's the realization of the dream for the Samaritan woman, for you, for me, and every other soul that meets His gaze—and keeps meeting it.

I picture you nodding your head at those words, because I find your writings full of encouragement that if we'll keep following the One we fell for, we'll continue to find more of Him to love. Thank you for that and for telling the Samaritan woman's story. There's so much to love about Jesus in this scene.

I marvel at the Inexhaustible God allowing Himself to feel weary and the Living Water allowing Himself to be thirsty, and then—be still my heart—being willing to ask for help from a woman. And not just any woman, but a woman your religious leaders would certainly call "unclean"—a woman the world was repeatedly using and discarding. I wonder what it was like for you and your friends to return and find Jesus in conversation with such a woman who, despite being "less-than" in the world's eyes, was being treated by Him as both worthy and welcome to inherit a place in His Kingdom!

Kudos to you for admitting it was a shocking moment, but no one had the nerve to ask Jesus why He was talking to her. That's the type of detail that makes me want to giggle. I'm a fan of those incidentals. It's saying something that no one, not even the characteristically brash Simon Peter, dared address. It makes me wonder if Jesus had a look on his face that said, *Don't even think about it.*

I used to give my kids that kind of look back in the day when I didn't want them to act like little monkeys in public. To be fair, John, I didn't want them to embarrass me, but I figure if Jesus had that kind of warning look on His face, He was concerned for the woman's feelings and not what anyone was thinking of Him. He was fiercely protective of her opportunity to have an encounter with Him and didn't want the spiritual atmosphere of that moment to be thrown off by other people. She was already wearing a ton of shame, already acutely aware of what everyone in her culture thought of her—and that's what drove her to the well in the heat of the day: avoidance. She was the town pariah. I say that because it fits with the overall tenderness of their exchange, and your friend Paul wrote that Jesus gave up all reputation in Heaven to come to Earth on His divine search-and-rescue mission. What a Savior!

It reminds me of that song I was telling you about. The lyrics end with the writer making the amazing discovery that the entire time he was looking for love, Love was looking for him. If you'll excuse me, I feel the need to sing that verse at the top of my lungs, and I might just toss in a line dance! (Yes, I'm going to sing, John. Be nice, and I'll teach you those dance steps when I get to Heaven. I might be vocally challenged, but I'm what some people might call a dancing machine!)

Hugs,
Shellie

Dear Reader,

As John 4 begins, we read that Jesus had to pass through Samaria on his way from Judea to Galilee. Bible scholars tell us there was, in fact, a second route between the two cities the Jews more commonly traveled so they could avoid passing through this Gentile town. And yet, Jesus had to pass through Samaria. Why? Because though He is the Savior of the entire world, He needed to orchestrate a meeting with this one Samaritan woman. Indeed, her exchange with Him led to the conversion of many in her hometown—but let's allow her story to encourage us in the tenaciously personal love Jesus has for each of us and the least of us. It has the distinction of being the lengthiest recorded conversation Jesus had with anyone during His earthly ministry, which seems all the more reason to lean in and listen.

[1] So then, when the Lord knew that the Pharisees had heard that [Jesus] was making and baptizing more disciples than John [2] (although Jesus Himself was not

baptizing; rather, His disciples were), [3] He left Judea and went away again to Galilee. [4] And He had to pass through Samaria. [5] So He came to a city of Samaria called Sychar, near the parcel of land that Jacob gave to his son Joseph; [6] and Jacob's well was there. So Jesus, tired from His journey, was just sitting by the well. It was about the sixth hour.

[7] A woman of Samaria came to draw water. Jesus said to her, "Give Me a drink." [8] For His disciples had gone away to the city to buy food. [9] So the Samaritan woman said to Him, "How is it that You, though you are a Jew, are asking me for a drink, though I am a Samaritan woman?" (For Jews do not associate with Samaritans.) [10] Jesus replied to her, "If you knew the gift of God, and who it is who is saying to you, 'Give Me a drink,' you would have asked Him, and He would have given you living water." [11] She said to Him, "Sir, You have no bucket and the well is deep; where then do You get this living water? [12] You are not greater than our father Jacob, are You, who gave us the well and drank of it himself, and his sons and his cattle?" [13] Jesus answered and said to her, "Everyone who drinks of this water will be thirsty again; [14] but whoever drinks of the water that I will give him shall never be thirsty; but the water that I will give him will become in him a fountain of water springing up to eternal life."

[15] The woman said to Him, "Sir, give me this water so that I will not be thirsty, nor come all the way here to draw water."

Jesus is on mission from the moment the woman approaches the well, and He wastes no time in breaking the culturally accepted rules of engagement between them. As a Jew, He wasn't supposed to socialize with women, and he certainly wasn't supposed to acknowledge a Samaritan woman. He does both, and it put the woman on high alert. I wonder if she proceeded cautiously because she suspected a trap. She wouldn't have been the first human to fear Jesus had an ulterior motive. Nor was she the last. I remember being suspicious about what Jesus wanted from me, too. Thankfully, He has proven incredibly patient in teaching me that what He wants most is to give me what I need the most, despite my persistent inability to identify it.

Jesus begins to beckon this woman toward an overflowing spring that will satisfy her soul and be an ever-flowing fountain of eternal life. She confuses His offer with the promise of plentiful physical water that would free her from these tiresome trips to the well and ease her day-to-day life. The disciples struggled with a similar misunderstanding. They repeatedly confused the reign of peace Jesus promised to bring to men's hearts with the physical kingdom they wanted him to establish in their land.

Grab a mirror, friend. You and I still suffer from similar confusion.

For example, we've already noted that our world is growing increasingly antagonistic toward believers. It's easy for us to get twisted, expecting God to validate us and right the wrongs against us while forgetting that our cause should be His, and that Jesus came to seek and to save lost souls. I wholeheartedly believe we're meant to engage in public discourse, but if the peace of Jesus isn't ruling in us, we'll be motivated by fear and we'll have nothing of eternal value to offer our broken world. I'm proposing a better way: we can watch our anxieties lose their grip by drinking from the Source of life as we're living it, and in doing so, we can model a life marked with contagious joy—by divine design.

Having held out to His new friend the promise of a dramatically different type of life and secured her interest in it, Jesus is about to show her the only thing that can keep her from experiencing it.

> [16] He said to her, "Go, call your husband and come here." [17] The woman answered and said to Him, "I have no husband." Jesus said to her, "You have correctly said, 'I have no husband'; [18] for you have had five husbands, and the one whom you now have is not your husband; this which you have said is true."

Ouch, right? Why did Jesus go there? Maybe He knew the Samaritan woman was wondering if He would rescind the invitation to this incredible Living Water if He really knew her. It'd be just like Jesus to answer the question before it's asked. *Yes,* He says to her. *Yes,* He says to us. *I know who you are and what you've done, and the offer stands. I'll give you eternal life if you'll own your sin and repent of it. I'll give you peace if you'll own your anxiousness and turn from it. I'll give you joy if you'll own your hopelessness and trust Me.*

Nicodemus had to give up his perceived righteousness, and the Samaritan woman had to face her ever-present shame. The two of them were poles apart socially, economically, and theologically, and yet equally distanced from their greatest need: Jesus. What a clear illustration of our human plight! None of us realize that Jesus is what we're longing for until He reveals Himself as our greatest need.

> [19] The woman said to Him, "Sir, I perceive that You are a prophet. [20] Our fathers worshiped on this mountain, and you people say that in Jerusalem is the place where one must worship." [21] Jesus said to her, "Believe Me, woman, that a time is coming when you will worship the Father neither on this mountain nor in Jerusalem. [22] You Samaritans worship what you do not know; we worship what we do know, because salvation is from the Jews. [23] But a time is coming, and even now has arrived, when the true worshipers will worship the Father in spirit and truth; for such people the Father seeks to be His worshipers. [24] God is spirit, and those who worship Him must worship in spirit and truth." [25] The woman said to Him, "I know that Messiah is coming (He who is called Christ); when that One comes, He will declare all things to us." [26] Jesus said to her, "I am He, the One speaking to you."

Without acknowledging that Jesus has read her mail, the Samaritan woman concedes that He is a prophet. But she's still unsure of what to do with Him, so she does what we all do when we can't get Jesus figured out: she falls back on the religion she's been taught and the comfortable controversies of the day. Jesus is having none of it. He dismisses what doesn't matter—which begs a question of today's Christ followers: What are we debating and allowing to divide us that doesn't matter in light of eternity? Jesus will tell us if we'll listen!

The only tension Jesus acknowledges exists in the reality of our earthly journeys—the dash between the hour that is coming and now is. Our religious institutions are tools at best. Jesus was asking the Samaritan woman to thrill to the Truth of God as revealed by the One speaking to her on His behalf: Christ, the Messiah, gift of God. And God is looking for worshipers today who will cling single-mindedly and wholeheartedly to Jesus, guzzle His grace, and give it away.

[27] At this point His disciples came, and they were amazed that He had been speaking with a woman, yet no one said, "What are You seeking?" or, "Why are You speaking with her?" [28] So the woman left her waterpot and went into the city and said to the people, [29] "Come, see a man who told me all the things I have done; this is not the Christ, is He?" [30] They left the city and were coming to Him.

[31] Meanwhile the disciples were urging Him, saying, "Rabbi, eat." [32] But He said to them, "I have food to eat that you do not know about." [33] So the disciples were saying to one another, "No one brought Him anything to eat, did he?" [34] Jesus said to them, "My food is to do the will of Him who sent Me, and to accomplish His work. [35] Do you not say, 'There are still four months, and then comes the harvest'? Behold, I tell you, raise your eyes and observe the fields, that they are white for harvest."

Apparently, the Samaritan woman isn't the only one confused by Jesus's references to nourishment and refreshment. I'm not throwing stones. I can be as dimwitted as Jesus's dullest disciple, but verse 30 tells us the woman's testimony had already intrigued her townspeople, that many of them were headed their way, and all the while, the guys were urging Jesus to eat. I can almost see Jesus taking the nearest disciple gently by the head and turning his eyes toward the approaching crowd. The missed meal is temporary. The people headed their way will live forever with, or separated from, Him.

The opportunity before them all was to stop wringing their hands about temporary things and turn their minds to an eternal harvest. Hello, Church! The world is rocking, but our knees aren't supposed to be knocking. We're set up in these turbulent days to bring in God's end-time harvest. We've been given access to joy in the midst of adversity that's meant to attract the world like moths to a flame. How? How can we move from handwringers to harvesters? Read on.

> [39] From that city many of the Samaritans believed in Him because of the word of the woman who testified, "He told me all the things that I have done." [40] So when the Samaritans came to Jesus, they were asking Him to stay with them; and He stayed there two days. [41] Many more believed because of His word; [42] and they were saying to the woman, "It is no longer because of what you said that we believe, for we have heard for ourselves and know that this One truly is the Savior of the world."

Many believed and begged Jesus to stay and teach them. And then many more believed. Their explanation is everything. They had heard Jesus for themselves. This is the answer to how we can believe and keep believing, too. We must hear Jesus for ourselves, again and again.

Hearing others tell us of Jesus can draw us to Him, and it's good to continue learning from the teachings of men. God gave us pastors and teachers (and bloggers, and podcasters, and influencers.) But continuing to marinate in His Word and listening for His Voice for ourselves is how we keep believing in the good news of salvation that drew us to Jesus. When the ground is shaking beneath our feet, He confirms His Presence in our listening spirits by His Word. Let's pray.

Dear Jesus,

Thank you for the promises we find in the Samaritan woman's story. We struggle to believe we're welcome to come as we are to You, with all our baggage, and saturate ourselves in Your goodness when we have nothing to offer and everything to gain. We struggle to accept that You know the past sin that shames us and the present sin that ensnares us, and still You keep calling us into the only relationship that can heal our choice-challenged souls. We're slow to understand that this Truth is the Living Water we can't afford to quit guzzling. Help us recognize that it is You we're thirsting for today, and then help us identify You as our greatest need again tomorrow! We won't live in that holy understanding without Your help. You're the Living Water we can't get enough of Who deeply satisfies us while simultaneously creating the sweetest longing for more of You. Bind us to You so we don't look at temporal sources for what You want to give us, the gift of Your Presence.

We confess that we like the world's approval, and being validated feels good, but we don't want to march to that pied-piper tune. It's an empty win. Help us remember the goal isn't to be proven right in this life, but to be proven faithful in it. As sorely as we need courage to confront evil in our day, we need wisdom to remember that Satan is the enemy, not the flesh-and-blood people who surround us. Give us eyes to see unbelievers as You see them: lost but beloved, in need of a Savior. Don't let us be so blinded by their opinions or our agenda that a precious human harvest becomes victim to the clash between our camps.

Teach us to listen to Your Word and look for the ways You're fulfilling it so that our faith might grow strong, and we may live extending hope to others. We offer these requests in Your precious and powerful name, Jesus. Amen.

For Discussion

1. The following passages record two other instances in the Bible where a woman meets either her future husband or his representative. Genesis 24:1–27 and 29:1–20. Read them and record the main characters by name. Jot down any similarities you might see in these accounts and the story of the Samaritan woman.

2. Shellie references Philippians 2:7–10 when suggesting that Jesus wasn't worried about being seen talking to the Samaritan woman. Read Hebrews 12:2. What does this verse tell us was motivating Jesus?

3. Read Genesis 28:16–19. Like so many other people in the Bible, and just like us, Jacob and the Samaritan woman were both slow to realize that God had drawn near. Do you think you and I can long for Jesus even though He is near? Do you see a solution in John 6:26 for this tendency? If so, what might it be?

CHAPTER FIVE

Recognize That Jesus's Cure
Is in His Command

D ear John,
 I met a man the other day I can't seem to forget, and that's fine. I want to keep remembering him in my prayers. To be clear, I didn't actually meet him. He was with a group I imagined to be his family, and I was with my husband, our grandson, and one of Weston's little friends. Since I didn't get the stranger's name, we'll call him Mr. Lost Man. That's the word he had tattooed inside his ear, John: LOST. It's what drew my attention to him. Granted, he had numerous tats, but it was his choice to have the word LOST printed on his body, inside his *ear*, that startled me.

 I wanted to talk to him, but I couldn't figure out how to step into the midst of his family and friends and blurt out what was on my mind. *"Excuse me, but I couldn't help noticing you have the word LOST tattooed inside your ear..."* It was hard to see that intro leading us into a good conversation, even though my concern was genuine. John, I didn't think badly of Mr. Lost Man. I *felt* badly for him.

I've tried to imagine the scenarios that would lead someone to tattoo LOST inside his ear. Even if he wasn't referring to his soul, even if he believes this world is all there is, it feels like such a sad self-revelation. Here's what I wish I would've said to him.

Mister, you don't have to be lost. The God who made you loves you with an everlasting love and He is calling for you. He'll leave a crowd of found people to bring you home, too!

You're ahead of me, aren't you? I imagine you're already recalling Jesus's words,

> "What man among you, if he has a hundred sheep and has lost one of them, does not leave the other ninety-nine in the open pasture and go after the one that is lost, until he finds it? And when he has found it, he puts it on his shoulders, rejoicing." (Luke 15:4–5)

We both know Jesus would've looked Mr. Lost Man square in the eyes and invited him to come home. I, on the other hand, can still be a big chicken about those kinds of public opportunities, as illustrated by my story. But hey, I've noticed I'm getting bolder. Spending time with Jesus will do that to a person. Amen? I watched you grow more fearless as you journeyed with Him, too. I have more to say about that, but right now I want to talk about the lame man at the pool of Bethesda.

I mean this in the nicest way, but I'd love more details on that story. I'm sure it's a female thing. (So says my darling husband who is notorious for hitting the high points and leaving me hungry for specifics. Bless him.) For the record, I realize everything I need to know in order to walk this faith life out is laid down in the Scriptures, but it doesn't seem to stop me from wondering about what isn't said.

For instance, the lame man's story is another one that's unique to your gospel. As I told you earlier, that exclusivity alone intrigues me, but even more so this time. Historians tell us that of the four gospels, you wrote yours last. So you knew the other guys didn't mention the lame man's healing at the Pool of Bethesda? Interesting. That means you also knew none of them had addressed the popular legend of your day that said an angel periodically stirred the waters to kick off a sad competition between the sick and lame. Reportedly, the first one in the pool after the stirring would be miraculously healed. Isn't that how it went? Just wow. Toying with sick people and selecting random winners? Doesn't sound like God to me—which brings me to something I found in my research.

There are Bible scholars who believe you, John, didn't actually include that ancient angelic detail found in verse 4. They think it was added to your gospel later by a well-meaning scribe. I suppose that could make some people nervous about the validity of God's Word, but it only serves to reassure me of its trustworthiness! Funny, huh? Let me explain. I find it extremely faith-building to know the Bible has survived centuries of endless textual comparisons between all the recognized manuscripts without yielding anything more than this type of rare discrepancy and without unearthing a single variance that contradicts or undermines the basic Gospel.

That sound you just heard was me taking a deep, long breath, John. The tested and tried Word of God offers soul-steadying confidence in our shaky world where "truth" is whatever a person wants it to be, and facts are often determined by those with the most power. Cover to cover, the Bible is a gift to be trusted and treasured. To that end, I'm grateful you had the courage to tell us about the lame man, curious-angel-backstory notwithstanding. Without it, we wouldn't have that deeply personal question from Jesus, "Do you want to get well?"

That heartfelt inquiry has helped many of us face the mirrors hanging on the walls of our homemade hideouts. It's encouraged us to break communion with the deadly self-pity that loves to masquerade as our comforting ally. In the lame man's story, we see Jesus respond to the man's reasoning of why he can't get well with the clearest command to "Get up, pick up your pallet and walk"—and those divine words have put the strength back into our legs to carry us into futures we couldn't see before He spoke into our lives, either.

So, thank you, John. Thank you for always revealing the heart of Jesus, our Life-Giver and our Light.

Hugs,
Shellie

Dear Reader,

It's okay if your Bible translation doesn't include verse 4 of John 5 or if it includes the curious angel legend with an asterisk and an explanation. The lame man's story has plenty to teach us without it. Jesus doesn't even address the guy's sad protest that the only reason he is still lame after thirty-eight years is because he can't move quickly enough to win the stirring-water lottery. Instead, Jesus responds to his sense of hopelessness, and He is here to respond to ours. Read the following passage and then meet me below.

> [1] After these things there was a feast of the Jews, and Jesus went up to Jerusalem. [2] Now in Jerusalem, by the Sheep Gate, there is a pool which in Hebrew is called Bethesda, having five porticoes. [3] In these lay a multitude of those who were sick, blind, limping, or paralyzed, [4] waiting for the moving of the waters; for an angel of the Lord went down at certain seasons into the pool and stirred up the water; whoever then first stepped in after the stirring up of the water was made well from whatever disease with which he was afflicted. [5] Now a man was there who had been ill for thirty-eight years. [6] Jesus, upon seeing this man lying there and knowing that he had already been in that condition for a long time, said to him, "Do you want to get well?" [7] The sick man answered Him, "Sir, I have no man to put me into the pool when the water is stirred up, but while I am coming, another steps down before me." [8] Jesus said to him, "Get up, pick up your pallet and walk." [9] Immediately the man became well, and picked up his pallet and began to walk.

There's a holy sequence in those verses we'd do well to embrace. Jesus tells the man to do what the man can't do, and when the man moves to do it, he discovers that he can! In other words, the cure was in Christ's command. If we'll move when Jesus speaks, He'll do through us what we could never do without Him. Let's keep reading.

> ⁹ Now it was a Sabbath on that day. ¹⁰ So the Jews were
> saying to the man who was cured, "It is a Sabbath, and
> it is not permissible for you to carry your pallet." ¹¹ But
> he answered them, "He who made me well was the one
> who said to me, 'Pick up your pallet and walk.'" ¹² They
> asked him, "Who is the man who said to you, 'Pick up
> your pallet and walk'?"

We aren't told whether these Jewish leaders witnessed the lame
man's healing. It's possible they simply saw him carrying his sleep-
ing bag on the Sabbath, which violated their rules, and they called
him on it. (Notice I said, "their rules," not "God's laws." We'll get
to that shortly.) Even if we give them the benefit of that doubt, their
hardhearted hypocrisy becomes glaringly obvious when the healed
man makes his defense. He reports that the one who healed him
told him to carry his bed, and their sole response is an indignant,
"Who would say such a thing?!" (My paraphrase.) I can't imagine
people being more concerned about their religion's rules than they
are the needs of the people it's meant to serve. Can you? (Yeah, that
made me wince, too.) The uncomfortable truth about church people
in our day is that we also can be preoccupied with protecting our
man-made traditions, and thus blinded to what God is doing.

Not so Jesus. He is repeatedly shown valuing people over religious precedent, and that love is on display as He follows up with
the man He healed.

> ¹³ But the man who was healed did not know who it was,
> for Jesus had slipped away while there was a crowd in
> that place. ¹⁴ Afterward, Jesus found him in the temple

and said to him, "Behold, you have become well; do not sin anymore, so that nothing worse happens to you." [15] The man went away and informed the Jews that it was Jesus who had made him well. [16] For this reason the Jews were persecuting Jesus, because He was doing these things on the Sabbath. [17] But He answered them, "My Father is working until now, and I Myself am working."

Kudos to the healed man for heading to the temple on his newly functional legs! And all praise to Jesus for searching him out for an eternally more significant follow-up. Jesus tells the man not to sin anymore so "nothing worse would happen" to him. I wonder whether Jesus was saying the man had been lame because of sin; I doubt it, because He was given numerous opportunities to yoke sin with physical sickness, and each time, He refused to make that kind of blanket connection. (We'll look at one such instance in John 9.) What Jesus did emphasize often is that sin separates man from God. This is the worse fate Jesus wanted to keep the man from experiencing, and it's the fate He wants to rescue you and me from, too.

The late Scottish poet and minister George MacDonald once noted that in the miracles of Jesus, we see Him doing instantly what His Father is doing constantly. Reading the gospels with that thought in mind produces one faith-fortifying discovery after another. Rest assured, Jesus looks out for us after our broken souls are healed of disbelief as surely as He looked for this man after his physical healing.

Jesus encourages us to keep coming, believing, and obeying because He hates the ravages of sin, and He knows His cure for our lives lies in His commands for us. He wants us to listen and obey so

He can lead us out of temptation and into abundant life. His words on working because His Father is working bring to mind the lyrics of a precious worship song: "Even when I don't see it, He's working."

The Jewish leaders were always accusing Jesus of breaking the Sabbath, when in reality, He was merely ignoring their handed-down traditions. Over time, the Jews had added more than four hundred rules to God's Law, and their tedious commands were overburdening the people. Jesus intentionally ignored these man-made add-ons because they were draining life from people, and He came to give it.

> [18] For this reason therefore the Jews were seeking all the more to kill Him, because He not only was breaking the Sabbath, but also was calling God His own Father, making Himself equal with God. [19] Therefore Jesus answered and was saying to them, "Truly, truly, I say to you, the Son can do nothing of Himself, unless it is something He sees the Father doing; for whatever the Father does, these things the Son also does in the same way. [20] For the Father loves the Son and shows Him all things that He Himself is doing; and the Father will show Him greater works than these, so that you will be amazed."

To an angry mob of power-drunk leaders already bristling from His refusal to abide by their rules, Jesus's claim to be one with God was like throwing gas on a fire. Did Jesus soothe them, appease them, apologize to them? Hardly. He doubled down and announced that greater works were coming than the ones currently rocking their world. Let's listen as He elaborates.

[24] "Truly, truly, I say to you, he who hears My word, and believes Him who sent Me, has eternal life, and does not come into judgment, but has passed out of death into life. [25] Truly, truly, I say to you, a time is coming and even now has arrived, when the dead will hear the voice of the Son of God, and those who hear will live. [26] For just as the Father has life in Himself, so He gave to the Son also to have life in Himself; [27] and He gave Him authority to execute judgment, because He is the Son of Man."

Jesus announced that God the Father sent Him to be both Life-Giver and Judge, and the one who hears Him has passed from death into life. "Has passed" is a present-tense resurrection, far greater than the healing of any physical body. Jesus welcomes us into His life, beginning now, and the reality of that invitation is a game-changing upgrade from what we've been conditioned to think of as eternal life once our eyes close on Planet Earth. When we live listening to Jesus, we can experience peace when others are panicking, and we can know joy that surpasses anything the world is chasing. It's when we decide we're too busy to lend our ears to Truth that we put ourselves at the mercy of the latest culture clash and the next round of breaking news.

With this announcement that a person could pass from judgement into life even as they were listening to His Voice, Jesus contradicted the Jews' merit-based religion that said people would be judged worthy or unworthy of gaining Heaven in the afterlife by how well they kept the Law. The crowd listening to Jesus realized He was saying that apart from Him, they were dead men walking, both now and later. Jesus's next words suggest the religious leaders were shocked by such an idea, and their astonishment was written on their faces.

> [28] "Do not be amazed at this; for a time is coming when all who are in the tombs will hear His voice [29] and will come out; those who did the good deeds to a resurrection of life, those who committed the bad deeds to a resurrection of judgment. [30] I can do nothing on My own. As I hear, I judge; and My judgment is righteous, because I do not seek My own will, but the will of Him who sent Me."

Jesus chose God's will over His own. We'll revisit that truth in the coming chapters. For now, let's stay in the moment and hear the witnesses Jesus offered as proof of His ability to deliver on everything He was promising.

> [31] "If I alone testify about Myself, My testimony is not true. [32] There is another who testifies about Me, and I know that the testimony which He gives about Me is true. [33] You have sent messengers to John, and he has testified to the truth. [34] But the testimony I receive is not from man, but I say these things so that you may be saved. [35] He was the lamp that was burning and shining, and you were willing to rejoice for a while in his light. [36] But the testimony I have is greater than the testimony of John; for the works which the Father has given Me to accomplish—the very works that I do—testify about Me, that the Father has sent Me. [37] And the Father who

sent Me, He has testified about Me. You have neither
heard His voice at any time nor seen His form. [38] Also
you do not have His word remaining in you, because you
do not believe Him whom He sent. [39] You examine the
Scriptures because you think that in them you have
eternal life; and it is those very scriptures that testify
about Me; [40] and yet you are unwilling to come to Me
so that you may have life."

Jesus reminded his accusers of how they had initially thrilled
to the testimony of John the Baptist—until the Baptist witnessed
to Jesus being the One sent from God. Next, Jesus pointed to the
testimony of His miraculous works that spoke of the Father's witness. Nicodemus, remember, had said the quiet part out loud when
he came to Jesus and confessed on behalf of his peers, "My friends
and I know you're from God because of the miracles you're doing."
(My paraphrase.) Finally, in what may have been the hardest thing
to swallow for those who prided themselves on knowing the Law
backward and forward, Jesus reminded those opposing Him that
He fulfilled the testimony of the Scriptures they were so fond of
searching.

We're about to hear Jesus explain to the religious leaders why
they couldn't believe. If you and I are serious about learning how
to believe and keep believing despite our post-Christian world, we
should pay very close attention to the following teaching.

[44] "How can you believe, when you accept glory from
one another, and you do not seek the glory that is from
the one and only God? [45] Do not think that I will accuse

you before the Father; the one who accuses you is Moses, in whom you have put your hope. [46] For if you believed Moses, you would believe Me, for he wrote about Me. [47] But if you do not believe his writings, how will you believe My words?"

Jesus says they couldn't believe because they sought glory from each other and didn't seek the glory that is from the one and only God. I remember when those words jumped off the holy page. I took them as a personal warning. I suggest you do the same: Seeking glory (approval) from people makes it more difficult for us to hear and believe God. Full stop.

It's okay if you're thinking about social media right now. That's a part of it. But we can fall into the trap of looking for man's affirmation offline, too. Perhaps we seek validation from our professional peers, or in being recognized as a good parent, a knowledgeable gardener, a dependable volunteer, etc. The list of ways we seek glory from flesh-and-blood people are as individual as we are, and they all hinder our ability to believe in God. Let's learn to recognize this ever-present snare and live asking the Lord to help us avoid it. Will you pray with me?

Dear Jesus,

You told the lame man to walk out of a condition he had deemed hopeless. We want to learn from his example and apply it. Help us believe that You don't ask us to do anything You won't equip us to do. Your cure is always in Your command. We know this and yet we confess that when it comes to obedience, we're prone to trying to will ourselves right with You and warrant Your assistance by our performance. Help us remember that the power to walk out of whatever is crippling our souls doesn't lie in our determination to get better, think better, or act better, but in listening and walking more closely with You, and relying more fully on Your indwelling Spirit.

Thank you for the gift of eternal life! It's sweet comfort to know our Judge is also our Redeemer. You've stacked the deck for us. We believe You are our Life-Giver, beginning now.

We acknowledge that we need You in this moment every bit as much as we needed You the day we first believed. Help us cling to this truth and draw daily encouragement from You to live courageous lives that testify of the change You've made in us!

We want to be lights for those who walk in darkness, but our own faith falters when we look to the world for approval and affirmation. Save us from that vicious pit. We make these requests in Your name and standing in Your favor. Amen.

For Discussion

1. Let's discuss John 5:4 and the angel legend that has been long debated among scholars. Read 1 Kings 19:1–8 and Acts 12:1–10. How do you feel the angels in these accounts are similar or different than the one at the center of this legend? What conclusions do they lead you to draw about the angel legend?
2. In response to the Pharisees' admonishment for carrying his bed on a Sabbath, the man who had been healed pointed to the One who healed him. Passages

like Titus 2:7–8 and Acts 5:29 offer direction on how we believers should conduct ourselves. Do you see this man as being courageous when the rulers confronted him? Do you interpret his response as merely being respectful of their authority? Or do you think he was "throwing Jesus under the bus"? (No wrong answers here.) Record any details you see in the story that might support your reasoning.

3. Reread John 5:25. Now, read Luke 15:24, Ephesians 2:1–5 and 5:14, and Colossians 2:13. After considering all these passages, do you think the dead who hear and live referred to in John 5:25 are physically or spiritually dead? Please explain your reasoning.

CHAPTER SIX

Fight for Your Faith by Feasting on the Word

D ear John,
     Back in elementary school, we had exams called "open-book tests." Our teacher would actually allow us to open our text-books to find the answers. What's more, she would encourage us to take our time to find the answers! I remember thinking there must be a catch. It seemed too good to be true. I half expected her to cry, "Gotcha!" at any moment and send us to the principal's office for cheating. It never happened, not even once. For the life of me, I couldn't see how anyone could fail an open-book test, but a few of my classmates always managed to surprise me.

     I've decided following Jesus can be like an open-book test, John, only infinitely better. God gives us His Word and encourages us to look in it for answers to all of life's questions. In my simplistic analogy, the infinitely better part is how God gives top grades to those who believe in Jesus before we even begin the test! Grace, grace—that's amazing grace, and it encourages me on the days when I seem to be failing the open-book test, which happens more than I care to admit.

Aren't we thankful for our long-suffering Teacher? I don't know how many times I read your gospel before it began to hit me. You and your friends struggled to grasp who Jesus was and what He was doing in your midst, despite the fact that y'all started following Him from the first day He said, "Come." Y'all were slow to catch on, and Jesus was right there in flesh and blood. Why, you could've pinched him! (You didn't, did you? Tell me you didn't pinch Jesus.)

I hope that early struggle isn't a sore subject. It's just that I figure you and Jesus must've enjoyed a few laughs about it by now, and I'm forever indebted to you for documenting your journey so openly. And not because it makes me feel superior, but because I get it! Jesus has taught my heart to love Him and I'm following Him as closely as I can, and I can still find myself entertaining doubts about Him. It grieves me so. It's also embarrassing, but I'm willing to put the following testimony out there in hopes it can help anyone reading my words the way your written account has so often helped me.

John, once I began to understand that y'all had a learning curve just like me, I started reading the Word differently. I began to see Jesus with fresh eyes, and what I saw has only deepened my love for Him! Here's what I learned that I now live to share with His other kids: During His stay here, Jesus was stern and unrelenting with those who refused to believe, but He showed incredible patience with those who trusted and followed Him, even when their comprehension was slow on the uptake. Grasping that good news is helping me seize the good life!

That patient side of Jesus, the Masterful Teacher, is on full display in your story of Him multiplying the young man's lunch to feed the five thousand. You wrote that Jesus tested Philip by asking him where you all could buy enough bread to feed all the people, even though He knew what He was going to do. Seriously, that was something of an open-book test, wasn't it? Y'all had watched Him turn water into wine, heal the centurion's son, and fix the lame man's legs. Philip could've said, "I don't know how you're going to feed them, Jesus, but I know you can do it!" Only, he didn't. You didn't say whether Philip looked to y'all for direction before answering, but in my imagination, no one would meet his gaze because none of you saw the whole fish fry happening. Am I close?

By the way, John, I realize the fish wasn't fried. My research tells me it was more likely smoked or cured. My people prefer hot grease and cornmeal with tartar sauce on the side. I think you would, too! I could fry you up some when I get to Heaven. Ask around and see if anyone has a Fry Baby. I'll see you sooner rather than later.

Hugs,
Shellie

Dear Reader,

As I mentioned to John, Philip probably should've had a better answer for Jesus as to how the crowd could get their bellies filled. But you and I get it, don't we? We have a difficult time trusting Jesus to meet our needs or solve our problems if we can't see how it's going to happen, even if we've already seen His faithfulness. For example, one of the things we can fear the most when we look at

our post-Christian culture is the effect it's having and will have on
our kids and grandkids. We wonder if we can turn the tide—and
what the future will be like for them if we can't. John's next story
is packed with courage for our wobbly knees.

> [1] After these things Jesus went away to the other side of
> the Sea of Galilee (or Tiberias). [2] A large crowd was fol-
> lowing Him, because they were watching the signs which
> He was performing on those who were sick. [3] But Jesus
> went up on the mountian, and there He sat with His
> disciples. [4] Now the Passover, the Feast of the Jews, was
> near. [5] So Jesus, after raising His eyes and seeing that a
> large crowd was coming to Him, said to Philip, "Where
> are we to buy bread so that these people may eat?" [6] But
> He was saying this only to test him, for He Himself knew
> what He intended to do. [7] Philip answered him, "Two
> hundred denarii worth of bread is not enough for them,
> for each to receive just a little!" [8] One of His disciples,
> Andrew, Simon Peter's brother, said to Him, [9] "There is
> a boy here who has five barley loaves and two fish; but
> what are these for so many people?" [10] Jesus said, "Have
> the people recline to eat." Now there was plenty of grass
> in the place. So the men reclined, about five thousand in
> number.
>
> [11] Jesus then took the loaves, and after giving thanks
> He distributed them to those who were reclining; like-
> wise also of the fish, as much as they wanted. [12] And
> when they had eaten their fill, He said to His disciples,

"Gather up the leftover pieces so that nothing will be lost." [13] So they gathered them up, and filled twelve baskets with pieces from the five barley loaves which were left over by those who had eaten. (John 6)

Mark tells this same story in his gospel, with an interesting prologue. Mark records that just prior to this mountain-feeding miracle, Jesus had sent the disciples out on their debut preaching tour. It was when they returned telling Jesus "all they had said and done" that Jesus encouraged them to come away with Him to a secluded place and rest awhile (Mark 6:30–31). The way I see it, the disciples were hyped! While exhausted from their ministry efforts, they were feeling good about their results, and that can be a dangerous place for any mortal. It's time for class to resume.

John opens his account by telling us a huge crowd followed Jesus to this mountain because of the healings he'd been performing. The stage is set in our not-so-secluded place with Jesus and His "rock star" disciples. We might not feel like we're slaying this Christian walk, but if the disciples needed the forthcoming object lesson, we can trust there's wisdom for us here, too.

Again, it's Mark who lets us know Jesus began the lesson by feeding the crowd for hours with His teachings because He felt compassion for them, recognizing them as sheep without a Shepherd. To be sure, the Bread of Life was holding them so spellbound that no one was making dinner plans when the disciples checked their watches and politely interrupted Jesus's sermon to notify Him of the time. (Raise your hand if you've ever acted like Jesus doesn't understand "the real world." Right, me neither.)

Jesus quickly takes the guys to the end of their reasoning, their resources, and their reputations. Imagine the disciples instructing thousands of people to sit down in small groups for a meal no one can see while Jesus held the sole lunch they'd been able to scrounge up: a bit of bread and a few small fishes. Do you suppose they felt powerless and maybe a bit foolish? They're now positioned to learn, and so are we.

The Bread of Life multiplies in Jesus's hands, not ours. Our families aren't at the mercy of a world that never has and never will be able to give them what they need! And we can't give them what they need, either, apart from Jesus. But, praise God, we can offer them overcoming life through Him! We can find nourishment in His hands for our own shaky souls and abundant supernatural food to share with our loved ones when we live by going back to Him for more.

In our next passage, Jesus will meet his disciples in the middle of a nightmare to underscore the same message. Whatever challenge we're facing, we're up to it if we are in Him, because He is more than enough.

[16] Now when evening came, his disciples went down to the sea, [17] and after getting into a boat, they started to cross the sea to Capernaum. It had already become dark and Jesus had not yet come to them. [18] In addition, the sea began getting rough, because a strong wind was blowing. [19] Then, when they had rowed about [three or four miles], they saw Jesus walking on the sea and coming near the boat; and they were frightened. [20] But he said to them, "It is I; do not be afraid." [21] So they were

willing to take Him into the boat, and immediately the
boat was at the land to which they were going.

It was dark, the water was rough, the situation felt dire, and
Jesus had not come to their rescue. How often have you been
there? Are you there right now? John doesn't include Peter's
water-walking moment, but this is where that famous story
occurred. Many sermons have been preached about getting out
of the boat and keeping your eyes on Jesus, but I don't think Jesus
was giving the disciples a tutorial on water walking, and I don't
think He's interested in us learning to defy gravity. The lesson we
need is that the peace we crave is found in understanding Who is
in the storm with us.

We want this stormy world to stabilize, but God wants to give
us a far more eternal treasure. He wants us to experience Immanuel,
God with Us, even as our circumstances pitch and roll. Jesus promised us tribulation in this world (John 16:33). As long as we take
promises meant for our souls and try to apply them to our every
physical situation in an effort to live untouched by this life's trials,
we'll continue to feel abandoned. But when we choose to trust that
Jesus is with us in them, we'll find Him faithful to calm our hearts
as surely as He did the seas. Will it be easy to believe this way? No.
Jesus says it will be work.

> 25 And when they found Him on the other side of the sea,
> they said to Him, "Rabbi, when did you get here?"
> 26 Jesus answered them and said, "Truly, truly, I say to
> you, you seek Me, not because you saw signs, but because
> you ate some of the loaves and were filled. 27 Do not work

for food that perishes, but for food that lasts for eternal life, which the Son of Man will give you, for on Him the Father, God, has set His seal." [28] Therefore they said to Him, "What are we to do, so that we may accomplish the works of God?" [29] Jesus answered and said to them, "This is the work of God, that you believe in Him whom He has sent."

We don't hear much teaching on the work of believing, but Jesus had no problem putting it out there. His next words tie our hope of sustaining such a work to feasting on Him as we're laboring to believe.

[35] Jesus said to them, "I am the bread of life; the one who comes to Me will not be hungry, and the one who believes in Me will never be thirsty."

As surely as physical bread sustains physical life, Jesus proclaimed Himself to be the Bread that sustains our born-again spirits. His audience couldn't accept that message, but Jesus ignored their protest to explain why they were resisting Him. It's a hard truth that comes with an important promise.

[43] Jesus answered and said to them, "Stop complaining among yourselves. [44] No one can come to Me unless the Father who sent Me draws him; and I will raise him up on the last day. [45] It is written in the Prophets: 'AND THEY SHALL ALL BE TAUGHT OF GOD.'"

If you have come to Christ, it's because God the Father drew you. Give thanks for the One who loved first, and then ask yourself the big question that comes with that promise. Is God teaching you? Is He teaching me? Do we go to Jesus for Bread, or do we go to man for leftovers? Again, teachers are God-given and necessary. It's biblical to learn in community and we're wise to do so, but giving up our own place at the table of the Bread of Life severely limits our experience of the New Covenant's blessings.

The crowd grumbled at Jesus's teaching, but He wouldn't be silenced. He reminded them that their ancestors ate manna from Heaven in the wilderness to ease their physical hunger, and they still died a physical death. In contrast, Jesus offered Himself yet again as the true Bread sent from God, that man might eat and never die. It was teaching they simply refused to accept. When they asked how Jesus could give them His flesh to eat, He spoke to their resistance, again.

[53] So Jesus said to them, "Truly, truly, I say to you, unless you eat the flesh of the Son of Man and drink His blood, you have no life in yourselves. [54] The one who eats My flesh and drinks My blood has eternal life, and I will raise him up at the last day. [55] For My flesh is true food, and My blood is true drink. [56] The one who eats My flesh and drinks My blood remains in Me, and I in him. [57] Just as the living Father sent Me, and I live because of the Father, the one who eats Me, he also will live because of Me. [58] This is the bread that came down out of heaven, not as the fathers ate and died; the one who eats this bread will live forever." [59] These things He said in the

synagogue as He taught in Capernaum. [60] So then many of His disciples, when they heard this, said, "This statement is very unpleasant; who can listen to it?"

Was Jesus waiting for them to acknowledge that His teaching was hard? I don't know. But once they do, He unpacks His analogy.

[61] But Jesus, aware that His disciples were complaining about this, said to them, "Is this offensive to you? [62] What then if you see the Son of Man ascending to where He was before? [63] It is the Spirit who gives life; the flesh provides no benefit; the words that I have spoken to you are spirit, and are life. [64] But there are some of you who do not believe." For Jesus knew from the beginning who they were who did not believe, and who it was who would betray Him.

[65] And He was saying, "For this reason I have told you that no one can come to Me unless it has been granted him from the Father."

Jesus spoke directly to the offense He knew He was causing and explained that He was telling them His Words were the meal they needed to consume, not His body. He was offering His grumbling listeners grace and truth, Himself and His teaching. But they preferred grace (God's favor) without truth (God's rule.) We love the themes of redemption and eternal life, but we can also be found harboring the dangerous question, "Do we really have to live on His Words?" Heads up, friends. That query aligns us with those who chose not to follow Jesus after this fateful conversation. Their departure is noted in the last passage of this chapter.

> [66] As a result of this many of His disciples left, and would no longer walk with Him. [67] So Jesus said to the twelve, "You do not want to leave also, do you?" [68] Simon Peter answered him, "Lord, to whom shall we go? You have words of eternal life. [69] And we have already believed and have come to know that You are the Holy One of God."

Following Jesus brings us all to this place, eventually. We find ourselves challenged, offended, and puzzled by Him. Blessed is the one who compares life with Him to life without Him and asks, "To whom else will we go?" We stagger, we admit to our ignorance and confusion, but when we consider the One who has awakened us to the words of Life, we recoil from the very idea of leaving Him. This is the faith that discovers the joy of continuing to believe. Have you been there? Pray with me.

Dear Jesus,

We need Your help to keep believing when life is offering us so many reasons to doubt. The growing antagonism to You in our public square makes us feel helpless and hopeless about the future. It's hard to hold on to our confidence in You as we look at the rising violence and economic instability all around us. And the uncomfortable truth? It makes us want to build higher fences and hide from it all. We want to overstock our pantries and make our own plans with our own hands. Relying on You for refuge and provision scares us when we can't use our human reasoning to see how You're going to meet our needs and those of our families. And yet, we know You're trustworthy. Help our unbelief!

Help us love and hunger for Your Word because our faith in You grows stronger as we feast on You. There is inexhaustible Peace in You. Teach us to keep our minds stayed on You. Help us reach for You when crisis comes. Where we are weary, we ask You for strength. Where we are hopeless, we ask You to increase our faith.

Our desire is to live on Your words. We don't want to be those who turn back from You. We acknowledge that You are offering Yourself to us, and You are full of grace and truth. We want both! We thank You for Your loving favor, and we surrender to Your ways. Help us come to You daily for the power to live out these convictions. In Your sweet name we ask these things of You, trusting that You are near, and that You hear our prayers. Amen.

For Discussion

1. What lesson or lessons do you think Jesus could have wanted the disciples to take away from His multiplying the bread and fish they found, rather than simply producing a feast from scratch? (No wrong answers, but here are a couple passages to get you thinking: Matthew 25:14–30, Ecclesiastes 9:10).

2. Read Job 9:8, 38:16, and then Psalm 77:19. Considering that the disciples were well-versed in the Scripture we call the Old Testament, explain why you think this was the first time they bowed to Jesus.

3. Jesus was teaching the crowd about their spiritual hunger and thirst, but they struggled to get past the analogy He used of His flesh being food and His blood being drink. Read Numbers 21:5 and share your thoughts as to why Jesus may have used that imagery.

CHAPTER SEVEN

Own Your Ever-Thirsty Soul

Dear John,
 I've been thinking of how people in your day chose religion over the living, breathing Jesus. Again, while many things have changed since you were here, much stays the same. People are still choosing religion over Jesus. Not proud of it, but I've lived that way myself. Today, I'm eternally thankful Jesus rescued me from that trap, but I'm also grateful He left me with a holy fear of falling back into it. That consciousness guards my soul. I'm always asking Him to alert me any time I'm leaning on a Jesus Stuffy instead of drinking from the well. A Jesus Stuffy? I'll explain, but first a story.

My kids and grandkids have all grown up cuddling stuffed animals we call "stuffies." Our littles bond with these lovies, and they learn how to use them to soothe themselves. (Have I lost you?

I doubt you have a point of reference for giving kids stuffed animals, but try to go with it for now. I think you'll understand soon enough.)

Kennedy Lee is my youngest grandchild, the caboose of six. We call her either "Kenny" or "KenKen the Baby Friend." One Sunday after church, she and her family came to our house for lunch. Sometime later, we were enjoying our customary post-meal fellowshipping on full bellies when we were interrupted by a potential crisis. KenKen's naptime had arrived, and Honey was missing! Honey is KenKen's beloved stuffed giraffe. (Trust me, John. A missing Honey is a big uh-oh, which is why a search-and-recovery mission commenced with all hands on deck.) There'd be no nap for KenKen and little peace for the rest of us if her love-worn giraffe wasn't found.

Thankfully, Honey was located. Disaster averted. I have a picture in my smartphone showing one incredibly happy KenKen perched on my hip, clutching Honey by the throat and smiling ear to ear!

The thing is, John, as much as KenKen adores her stuffy, those of us who love her know all too well that a day is coming when KenKen's stuffy won't be enough to console her. We know she'll face challenges as she grows up that will demand more than a cuddly stuffed animal can offer. We know this because we're living in them.

As you know, life on Earth can be hard, even when it's good. These days, hard seems to be coming at us from all sides at once. In another of what we call "developments," we're treated to news from around the globe in real time. The world's sorrows pile in on top of the challenges that come with life itself. Can you even imagine? It means we get today's drama before we've had time to process yesterday's trauma. Add to that tension our society's broken relationship with truth. Everyone is a fact checker, but there's little consensus on whose facts can be trusted. It can all leave us feeling vulnerable on our best days, and desperate on our worst.

I'm having interactions with hopeless and anxious people on a scale I've never known before. Conversations can go from "How are you doing?" to "How do you know Jesus is real?" in a hot minute. Personally, I think it's because Jesus is coming soon and we're experiencing what He told you guys were "birth pains"—the world events that mark the beginning of His second coming. Of course, I have no idea how close we are to His return; no human does. But I'll tell you what I do know: I know about birth pains. I know they build until they culminate in a birth, and I know they don't go backward, regardless of how badly we might want them to. There were moments when I was birthing my first baby that I wanted to call the whole thing off and go back to how things used to be, too! But I digress.

Today, I hear people wondering if we'll ever go back to normal, or their idea of it. I think that's the wrong question for believers. I think we need to be asking how we can live joyfully and peacefully in the midst of these unsettling times in a way that points lost souls to Jesus. Amen?

This is where the "Jesus Stuffies" tie in, John. We churched people tend to make stuffies out of things like church attendance, worship music, devotionals, and our long-ago salvation experiences. Some of those are good spiritual disciplines, but apart from an abiding relationship with Jesus, they're all Jesus Stuffies—and Jesus Stuffies won't be enough for us in these times. Indeed, they never have been. Jesus Stuffies won't help us extend hope to the hopeless,

either. We need Jesus Himself. Right, John? Oh, for grace to hunger
for Him more.

Hugs,
Shellie

Dear Reader,

Remember the summer camp I told you I hold for my grands?
I mentioned it in the introduction. Camp commences with the
grands and I racing through a preplanned list of our favorite activities like it's our last hurrah, and camp concludes with the grands
planning the next blowout! It takes this Keggie a tad longer to even
think about holding another cousin-fest, but I get there. I always
get there. This kind of happy gathering where everyone knows
what's about to happen and enjoys it to the max anyway is the type
of celebration we see in the seventh chapter of John. I need to set it
up for you so we can squeeze every ounce of goodness from the
announcement Jesus makes at the peak of it!

This party was planned centuries earlier by God Himself
(Leviticus 23:41–43), and in His instructions, He literally commanded His kids to "be joyful at your festival" (Deuteronomy 16:14
NIV). I love a good be-happy commandment, and from all
accounts, the Hebrews embraced it, too. During this week-long fall
celebration known as *Sukkot* or "The Feast of Tabernacles," Jews
partied hard. They gave thanks for the latest harvest and asked God
to send rain for the next one, all while celebrating the history of
His provision and protection. Special emphasis was placed on the
years God cared for the young nation as they journeyed to the
Promised Land.

To remind the Jews of those long-ago days when He provided for their every need as they journeyed through the wilderness living in tents, God instructed each family to celebrate *Sukkot* by building temporary outdoor dwellings to use during the festival. *Sukkot* is the plural form of *sukkah*, which means "booth, hut, or tabernacle." Meals were taken in these structures throughout the week to commemorate those wilderness days when God tabernacled among them. Today, many Jewish families still celebrate *Sukkot* by building these outdoor structures, and many Israeli restaurants and hotels offer *sukkahs* during the holiday for their guests to enjoy.

During the festival, a priest would go daily to the Pool of Siloam, draw water, and bring it back to the temple. He would be followed by a crowd of festival-goers who played music, sang, and danced along the way. As the priest neared the altar of burnt offering, the crowd would begin yelling, "Lift up your hand! Lift up your hand!" This part of the tradition came about because of a rogue priest who once demonstrated his disrespect for the ritual by pouring the sacred water out at his feet! This chant was the crowd saying, "Not again! Not on our watch!" The priest would then empty the water into a bowl on the altar as a second priest poured wine into it and the people shouted, clapped, and sang words taken from the prophet Isaiah: "With joy will you draw water from the wells of salvation" (Isaiah 12:3 ESV).

To be sure, I've barely hit the high points of this shindig. Think of it as the party of the year! Jerusalem was overrun with festival-goers bent on enjoying a week of feasting, fellowship, and entertainment. For the Hebrews of Jesus's day who were living under Roman rule, this moment embodied their Messianic hopes. They held tightly to God's promise of a coming day when He would pour out the living water of His Spirit on them to renew their joy and restore their nation. All those hopes and dreams were captured in the daily outpouring of water from the priest's golden flask. Day after day, expectations of God's coming deluge built, resulting in a shared exuberance on the final day that prompted the people of ancient Israel to say, "If you had never seen this joyous moment, you have never seen rejoicing!"

That, friend, is the scene of the following passage:

> Now on the last day, the great day of the feast, Jesus stood and cried out, saying, "If anyone is thirsty, let him come to Me and drink. The one who believes in Me, as the Scripture said, 'From his innermost being will flow rivers of living water.'" (John 7:37–38)

BOOYAH!

Every single person hearing that clarion call would've understood exactly what Jesus meant by it. He was declaring Himself to be the promise they'd been waiting for: God's Living Water standing in their midst. His message? He could fulfill all their hopes and dreams if they would only come to Him and believe. In this poignant moment, Jesus was offering His listeners the same invitation He is extending to you and me: "Come to Me believing I am all you need, and I will be your supply of overflowing joy!"

It's a tailor-made invite for each of us, right where we are. Jesus doesn't say if a rich man or woman is thirsty, or a poor man or woman, and He doesn't limit His offer to a particular race. Thirst is the only qualification, and coming to Jesus is the only condition! If we own our thirst and come to Jesus, He will satisfy our souls. Jesus said the river of life He offered would not only quench the people's thirst; it would bubble up out of their lives. Are we concerned for our world, for our families, our friends? Our answer is to lay hold of Jesus. When He is nourishing our lives, the overflow of His Sprit will splash all over them. We can't deliver them to Jesus, but He can and will draw them through our lives.

Like the children of Israel in the wilderness, we too are pilgrims on this earth, but we aren't left to wander alone and confront the darkness by ourselves. Jesus is here to dwell with us.

> And the Word [Jesus] became flesh and dwelt among us.
> (John 1:14)

Listen to how John the Writer expounds on Jesus's living-water offer in the very next verse.

> But this He said in reference to the Spirit, whom those who believed in Him were to receive; for the Spirit was not yet given, because Jesus was not yet glorified. (John 7:39)

The Cross was straight ahead, and after it the resurrection, where Jesus was glorified and the promise of the Spirit was being given to all who believe.

Joy is our birthright. Living Water is available. As long as we own our thirst, we can bring our flagging joy to Jesus for a refill. Cheers to you, friend. Drink up!

Dear Jesus,

We, Your people, are a mess. We confess. We're so thirsty for You and so prone to not recognizing it or, worse still, ignoring it. We're experts at this. We have a way of marching on with dry throats, trying to say and do all the right things under the power of our own fatigued souls while we reach for quick fixes from this life that only exacerbate the problem. You know such living drains our souls and leaves us fatigued, vulnerable to the enemy's onslaught, fearful, and defenseless against the darkness. Help us grasp this truth so we will live drawing from Your Presence.

And while You're working that revelation into our hearts, Jesus, we ask You to reveal the root of the problem. It's not pretty, but You see our ugly and You stand ready to heal it. Show us the real reason why we can be so slow in bringing our thirsty hearts to You. Help us to admit that we aren't always convinced that what You're offering is what we need. It hurts to put it in black and white, but our only hope is to stop posturing with You as if we aren't faith challenged, when all the while our hearts are already laid open and bare before Your eyes. So, like the father of the demon-possessed child once did, we cry aloud to You, "We do believe, Jesus! Help our unbelief!"

We, Your sheep, are prone to wandering into dangerous places and drinking from sickly wells. Wean us from worldly mirages that can't fortify us. We're helpless without You, Great Shepherd, and we're ready to own what You know. We need You. Our joy is flagging. We're thirsty and dry. Fill us, Jesus, and keep us drinking from the well.

For Discussion

. . . .

1. Read Proverbs 10:11 and 18:4. How often would your circle of family and friends experience a fountain of life or bubbling brook in conversation with you? What verse here in the seventh chapter of John shows us how to move that needle in a positive direction?

2. Read Deuteronomy 32:36, paying special attention to what it has to say about our strength. Do you see any connection between this verse and the advantage of owning our neediness for Jesus as we've discussed it in this chapter?

3. Underline the promises of Isaiah 58:10–11 in your Bible or record them here. Now, read verses 1–9 of the same chapter. Discuss how God expects us to live as we're asking Him to replenish our souls. Do you see obligation or opportunity in this passage? Put your answer in the form of a prayer.

CHAPTER EIGHT

Embrace a Lifestyle of Repentance

Dear John,

Time has taught me just how blessed I was to grow up within the steady influence of a small rural community, anchored around the sound biblical teachings of Melbourne Baptist Church. But let me be honest. The tight-knit relationships I remember with fondness now seemed like more of a liability in my childhood.

Mama employed our whole extended community in her goal to keep my sisters and me on our best behavior. For instance, she didn't immediately jump to our defense if we got in trouble at church or school. She looked into the incident instead. If the discipline was warranted, we could expect additional punishment at home. Mama also had a way of reinforcing our lessons through public exposure, and she was good at her game! I rarely saw those traps coming. Without warning, she'd invite me into an adult conversation with a seemingly pleasant instruction. "Shellie, tell Dee Dot what you got yesterday."

Dee Dot was the nickname of Mama's good friend. She was also one of my favorite adults—and while Mama's request might sound pleasant enough, it meant me telling a story I didn't particularly relish sharing about whatever punishment I'd received from my latest lack of judgment. We girls have chided Mama for that questionable parenting technique over the years, to her amused indifference. Clearly, she felt it served her purpose at the time.

I mention this, John, to tell you the thing I remember most about those uncomfortable moments is the expression on Dee Dot's face as I rehearsed my misdeed. Her dark brown eyes were tender and encouraging. Though my guilt was a given, she'd respond with something like, "I bet you won't do that again"—and just like that, it was case closed.

Your story of the woman who was caught in adultery and brought to Jesus for judgment makes me think of Dee Dot. I imagine His expression to be something like hers, only immeasurably more compassionate because, of course, the stakes are far greater. I get that. Her moment of reckoning didn't follow a childhood misdemeanor. It held life-and-death consequences.

It doesn't sound like she pled her case with words, John, but was there a plea on her face? Could you even see her face? Perhaps she kept it bowed as her accusers set a trap for Jesus with her life as the bait. She knew what to expect. You all did.

What she couldn't have known was that Jesus was as familiar with the sins of those accusing her as He was with hers. She wouldn't have known He was about to evade the trap meant for His feet to set one for theirs. In my imagination, the woman's head is still lowered and she's quite possibly staring at the marks Jesus is penning in the dirt when she sees their sandaled feet retreating. I see her waiting until there is only one pair left before she looks up to see their owner and hears Him ask, *"Where are they? Has no one accused you?"* My heart thrills to His mercy-draped words that met her response, *"Neither do I condemn you. Go and sin no more."*

She was guilty, but she wasn't condemned.

I can't get enough of that. It helps me believe Jesus isn't turning away from the worst of me, either. His kindness to her quiets my insecurities. It gives me the courage to keep bringing my ugly to Him so He can keep teaching me how to live a new way, His way.

Oh, the love that must have shown from His eyes, John! I can't wait to see it for myself. How do you ever look at anything else? Or do you?

Hugs,
Shellie

Dear Reader,

We're about to read the familiar account of the woman caught in adultery. We most often use this passage to preach to each other about keeping our judgmental stones in our self-righteous pockets. That's valid, but this story has much more to offer. Take in the following verses and I'll meet you below.

[1] But Jesus went to the Mount of Olives. [2] And early in the morning He came again into the temple area, and

all the people were coming to Him; and He sat down
and began teaching them. [3] Now the scribes and the
Pharisees brought a woman caught in the act of adultery, and after placing her in the center of the courtyard,
[4] they said to Him, "Teacher, this woman has been
caught in the very act of committing adultery. [5] Now in
the Law, Moses commanded us to stone such women;
what then do You say?" [6] Now they were saying this to
test Him, so that they might have grounds for accusing
Him. But Jesus stooped down and with His finger wrote
on the ground. (John 8)

The scribes and Pharisees, those most knowledgeable about the
law, those who were always throwing it around, failed to recognize
Jesus as the author of it. So, they set out to trap Him with His own
words. We know something about gotcha moments, don't we?
Should we dare take to our keyboards to post an opinion, we can
count on the scrutiny police to be standing poised to parse it.
Furthermore, if we don't weigh in on the current outrage, we feel
the expectation to speak up rising from our like-minded circles,
and we can hear the clock ticking. Regardless of the size of our
influence, the trap is set.

Note the difference in Jesus's response. When His credentials,
His morals, and His judgement were all challenged, Jesus paused
and knelt. Actions really can be louder than words. What an
example! We need to speak up against evil, and our walk should
match our talk, but we'd do well to learn from the Master. Let's
pause and bow our hearts to God before responding.

[7] When they persisted in asking Him, He straightened up and said to them, "He who is without sin among you, let him be the first to throw a stone at her." [8] And again He stooped down and wrote on the ground. [9] Now when they heard this, they began leaving, one by one, beginning with the older ones, and He was left alone, and the woman where she was, in the center of the courtyard. [10] And straightening up, Jesus said to her, "Woman, where are they? Did no one condemn you?" [11] She said, "No one, Lord." And Jesus said, "I do not condemn you, either. Go. From now on do not sin any longer."

We can feel Jesus's compassion for the woman in this story, but what about her accusers? What did He feel for them? While we don't know what Jesus wrote in the dirt that day, we can know the desire of His heart for everyone present: that none would perish but all would come to everlasting life (2 Peter 3:9). Had any of the woman's accusers knelt in repentance, that soul would've found forgiveness.

Did you notice Jesus had parting words for the woman, but none for her accusers? Telling them to "sin no more" would be pointless when they hadn't owned their present sin. Jesus knows better than we do how powerless we are before the sin we keep hidden. Whatever He isn't Lord over in our lives will continue to lord it over us.

So, while clearly convicted, the men left with their sins still hidden, at least temporarily. On the other hand, the woman who was naked and exposed didn't seize the opportunity to run for cover. What in the world is happening here? I believe the woman saw her sin in light of her Savior and repented. I say that because Jesus pardoned her, and the Bible teaches that God can't forgive unless we repent.

> "No, I tell you, but unless you repent, you will all like-
> wise perish." (Luke 13:3)

There's yet another reason I suspect she may have repented. According to John 8:4, the accusers addressed Jesus as "Teacher." Look back at verse 11 and you'll hear the woman call Him "Lord." It might seem inconsequential, but it can make a critical difference. I say that because "Teacher" is a religious title that doesn't necessarily reflect a submissive heart in the person saying it. Acknowledging Jesus as Lord requires repentance. One is professional; the other is personal.

This repentance, this change of mind that impacts the way we live, isn't meant to be a once-and-done decision, but a lifestyle! Scripture reveals it as our only hope of becoming intimately acquainted with the One we've put our trust in and experiencing the transformation the Bible promises for believers. The biblical word for this present-tense metamorphosis is "sanctification." It simply means partnering with the Spirt of God to become increasingly more like Jesus. It's the Spirit continuing to correct and us continuing to respond, because conviction alone isn't repentance, and it doesn't lead to fellowship. Ask the Pharisees.

It's never easy to own our sin. Not at our conversion, and not in the many times the Holy Spirit convicts us as we grow afterward. And yet, the life-changing reward of repentance is fellowship with Jesus now, on this side of Heaven! By refusing to run for cover, the woman in our passage found herself alone with Him. There's no better company. The Bible speaks of God granting repentance (2 Timothy 2:25). See it for the gift it is. Embrace it and live in Jesus's stabilizing embrace.

Dear Jesus,

Help us learn to humble ourselves and listen for You before we take it upon ourselves to respond to others. Whether it's the news of the day we're itching to address or more personal relationships that tempt us to speak too quickly, we understand that our rash words are potentially damaging words. Your Word promises to guide us, but we can't hear Your instructions when we're talking. Give us ears to listen.

Your Word also teaches us that our tongues hold the power of death and life. Give us discernment when we do speak. These days, our phones make it easier than ever to hurl potent words at friends and family, at our next-door neighbor, and at people all around the world. Help us see that our typed-out words are just as damning or life-giving as the ones we say in person. Set a watch over our lips and our fingers. We want to speak life-giving words, and we want to write them, too. Don't let us sacrifice our call to win souls to our desire to win arguments.

Help us learn to see repentance for the life-giving, growth-fueling gift it is, and to practice it. We bring You our hearts today. Sweep everything into the open and reveal the sins that are entrapping us. Show us where we've been resisting Your correction. We

*know we can't hide from You, and we are done trying. Going
forward, we want to agree with You, repent before You, and live
in You. Jesus, we stand in Your gracious favor as we make these
requests in Your name. Amen.*

For Discussion

1. Read Proverbs 15:28 and 18:19. Compose a sentence
   or two stating any conviction you hear in these verses
   and how you intend to respond to that lesson going
   forward.

2. Read Exodus 20:14 and 31:18 and Deuteronomy 9:10.
   What connection do you see between those verses and
   John 8:6? Do you think the Pharisees missed it or
   willfully ignored it? Explain how your answer relates
   to responding to conviction or resisting it.

3. Read John 8:31–59. The people claiming to believe in
   Jesus in verse 31 are picking up rocks to stone Him by
   verse 59! There are several verses in between that
   might tell us why their superficial faith failed. Note
   one or more of these verses and explain why you think
   that happened.

CHAPTER NINE

Accept What You Can't Know, Act on What You Do

D^{ear} John,

Dear John,
    Let's talk about that fascinating day when Jesus put mud in the blind man's eyes. You said y'all were walking along when Jesus saw a blind man. Sounds like the discussion began because y'all followed His gaze to the sightless fellow. It must've seemed like a perfect opportunity to get an answer to the mystery of sin and suffering. I'm guessing that's why y'all gave Him a multiple-choice test on "whose sin caused the suffering." Only Jesus chose none of the above. That Jesus. He just refuses to be boxed in, doesn't He? For what it's worth, we're still asking why bad things happen, especially when it strikes those we think of as "good people." My daughter falls into this category. She said I could tell you her story.

Jessica Ann is a beautiful young woman. She's wife to Patrick and mother to Grant and Connor. For the last decade, Jessica has been on a mysterious health journey with a list of random symptoms, not the least of which are sustained weight loss and chronic pain. She was seen by countless experts to no avail—until 2020, when a cardiac surgeon concluded she had a rare condition known as Nutcracker Syndrome. (I had never heard of it, either!) For brevity's sake, John, it means two of Jessica's arteries are pressing together and pinching off her left renal vein, restricting blood flow from her kidney to her heart and leading to myriad other complications.

Jessica entered the hospital a few months later to have a stent placed in her compromised renal vein to hold it open so the blood could flow. And it did—initially.

My husband and I were in Houston, where Jessica and her family live, to care for the boys during the surgery and allow Patrick to be by her side. Her surgeon was delighted to show us an ultrasound of Jessica's abdomen taken before and after the stent was placed. Jessica's pelvic region and extremities were showing signs of increased blood flow. There was much thanksgiving! We notified praying friends and family, and took Jessica home.

This is when the story becomes hard to tell, John. This mama will need to hit the main points.

Within hours, Jessica's post-surgery pain and discomfort began mounting inexplicably. We notified her surgeon. Reasoning aloud, he told us the extreme pain she was describing could possibly mean the new renal stent was migrating—but since it'd been perfectly situated and he'd never had one migrate in the thousands of times he'd performed this surgery, he couldn't imagine it was happening now. Only it was.

By the time we got Jessica back into surgery, the stent was lodged in her heart. She was in surgery for six long and tedious hours while a team of professionals attempted to safely remove it. There's much I could say about that intervening wait before we got word the stent was out and Jessica was headed to recovery. I may be able to tell it all one day—just not today. I'd rather share the moment I finally got to see my daughter again.

I slipped into Jessica's hospital room, pushed back a privacy curtain, and met my firstborn's eyes. We didn't speak at first. We just held each other and cried. Then Jessica said something in a low whisper, her voice hoarse from intubation. It wrecked me then and it wrecks me now.

"I still love God," she said, *"but I'm mad at Him right now."*

I understood what she was saying and everything she wasn't.

Jessica has since told me it hasn't been easy to find her way back to talking to God, to trusting Him again through all the health scares. It's been a process. It's taken time. She's had to do it without getting an answer to her many questions—which brings me back to your story.

I think I see why Jesus didn't settle the debate about suffering that day. It's because we'll never be able to look at the mystery of suffering, wherever we find it, and accurately discern its cause. We're far better off trusting Jesus and watching to see how the suffering reveals God's glory. Am I close?

Thanks for listening, John. Until next time.

Hugs,

Shellie

Dear Reader,

John tells a story in the ninth chapter of his book about a man who'd been blind from birth. The disciples want to know whether he sinned or his parents did, because they'd been taught all suffering was the result of sin. Jesus refuses to address the cause and effect. He leaves the mystery of suffering on the table to announce instead that the power of God is about to be displayed in the blind man's life and to remind the disciples that He, Jesus, is the Light of the World.

That sliver of supernatural biographical information reaches beyond the blind man to you and me. Without Jesus, Light of the World, none of us can see God. Throughout Scripture, the physical eye is used to represent spiritual seeing or perception (Matthew 6:22–23, Ephesians 1:18). With that in mind, let's see what implications this story holds for us.

> [6] When He had said this, He spit on the ground, and made mud from the saliva, and applied the mud to his eyes, [7] and said to him, "Go, wash in the pool of Siloam" (which is translated, Sent). So, he left and washed, and came back seeing. (John 9)

John doesn't say why Jesus initiated this exchange with the blind man instead of the blind man reaching for Jesus. Maybe the man was resigned to his sightless life. Perhaps he didn't know who Jesus was, or he was unaware of His arrival. Regardless, once Jesus rubs mud on the man's eyes, the guy is open to further instruction. Mark that and consider our present situation. We may be resigned to the darkness of our world, but Jesus isn't okay with the status quo. He knows He is the Light, and He knows how badly we need Him. Jesus will allow us to feel desperation for our own good. Brace yourself: He'll even create it. Indeed, Jesus is willing to rub mud in our eyes to get us to respond and see Him for Who He is. He'll aggravate our condition to encourage us to seek grace. What a Savior!

Let's keep reading. As the story progresses, the man's spiritual eyesight will become clearer as he acts on what he begins to understand—brilliantly illustrating that obedience to what we know opens our understanding for more revelation.

> [8] So the neighbors, and those who previously saw him as a beggar, were saying, "Is this not the one who used to sit and beg?" [9] Others were saying, "This is he," still others were saying, "No, but he is like him." The man himself kept saying, "I am the one." [10] So they were saying to him, "How then were your eyes opened?" [11] He answered, "The man who is called Jesus made mud, and spread it on my eyes, and said to me, 'Go to Siloam and wash'; so I went away and washed, and I received sight." [12] And they said to him, "Where is He?" He said, "I do not know."
>
> [13] They brought the man who was previously blind to the Pharisees. [14] Now it was a Sabbath on the day that Jesus made the mud and opened his eyes. [15] Then the Pharisees also were asking him again how he received his sight. And he said to them, "He applied mud to my eyes, and I washed, and I see." [16] Therefore some of the Pharisees were saying, "This man is not from God, because He does not keep the Sabbath." But others were saying, "How can a man who is a sinner perform such signs?" And there was dissension among them. [17] So they

said again to the man who was blind, "What do you say about Him, since He opened your eyes?" And he said, "He is a prophet."

Let's review. The first time his astonished neighbors asked the newly sighted man how he came to see, he tells them a man named Jesus rubbed mud on his eyes; and then, when he washed the mud off at the pool of Siloam per the man's instructions, he could see. By the time the Pharisees begin to question him, Mr. I Can See has decided Jesus is no mere man, but a prophet. Refusing to believe any of his story, the indignant Pharisees call the man's parents to the hearing.

[19] And they questioned them, saying, "Is this your son, who you say was born blind? Then how does he now see?" [20] His parents then answered and said, "We know that this is our son, and that he was born blind; [21] but how he now sees, we do not know; or who opened his eyes, we do not know. Ask him; he is of age, he will speak for himself." [22] His parents said this because they were afraid of the Jews; for the Jews had already reached the decision that if anyone confessed Him to be Christ, he was to be excommunicated from the synagogue. [23] It was for this reason that his parents said, "He is of age; ask him."

[24] So for a second time they summoned the man who had been blind, and said to him, "Give glory to God; we know that this man is a sinner." [25] He then answered, "Whether He is a sinner, I do not know; one thing I do

know, that though I was blind, now I see." ²⁶ So they said to him, "What did He do to you? How did He open your eyes?" ²⁷ He answered them, "I told you already and you did not listen; why do you want to hear it again? You do not want to become His disciples too, do you?" ²⁸ They spoke abusively to him and said, "You are His disciple, but we are disciples of Moses. ²⁹ We know that God has spoken to Moses, but as for this man, we do not know where He is from." ³⁰ The man answered and said to them, "Well, here is the amazing thing, that you do not know where He is from, and yet He opened my eyes! ³¹ We know that God does not listen to sinners; but if someone is God-fearing and does His will, He listens to him. ³² Since the beginning of time it has never been heard that anyone opened the eyes of a person born blind. ³³ If this man were not from God, He could do nothing." ³⁴ They answered him, "You were born entirely in sins, and yet you are teaching us?" So, they put him out.

Talk about the light dawning! Mr. I Can See has come a long way in a short time. He's now willing to stand before his family, his community, and those in authority to insist that Jesus could not have healed him unless He came from God! That public profession and his resulting expulsion from temple fellowship draws the attention of Jesus, Son of God.

³⁵ Jesus heard that they had put him out, and upon finding him, He said, "Do you believe in the Son of Man?" ³⁶ He answered by saying, "And who is He, Sir,

that I may believe in Him?" [37] Jesus said to him, "You have both seen Him, and He is the one who is talking with you." [38] And he said, "I believe, Lord." And he worshiped Him.

Jesus came to find this man who was acknowledging Him and wanting to understand more. He is still coming for seekers. Take heart, Little Faith. Jesus doesn't come once we have it all figured out, because we won't ever do that. We can't. But He does come, over and again, to those who accept the mystery of all we don't know while reaching for more of the One who first opened our eyes.

As believers, you and I are no longer of this world, but we still live in it. We can experience the peace of God by accepting what we can't understand and acting on what we do. We can discover deeper joy by seizing this truth: Jesus, Light of the World, is faithful to grant increasing sight to all who walk in the light they've been given. Let's pray.

Dear Jesus,

We're prone to stopping so short of Your purposes for our lives. Thank You for loving us enough to make us desperate for more of You than we're experiencing. We realize You don't ask us to give thanks for hard things, but You are here to empower us to give thanks in and through them. Teach us such living.

Help us to hunger for more revelation of You, that we might be transformed by You, and so offer eternal hope to those around us. We confess what You know: complacency is our default. We're capable of resigning ourselves to the pain of others caused by the *devil's depravity and numbing ourselves to their horror, as long as we can make charitable, conscience-soothing forays into the darkness before hustling back to the little kingdoms we're curating for ourselves and our loved ones. Forgive us for our ugly, persistent self-centeredness. Form Yourself in us and teach us to love sacrificially.*

When You healed the blind man, He acknowledged You regardless of public opinion. Help us be that kind of courageous in our day. We don't have to be ashamed because we don't have all the answers. We're not called to explain suffering. We're called to trust You and seek Your glory. And we can, through the power of Your indwelling Spirit. Bind us to You.

Thank You for counting the great cost of the Cross and enduring it, that we might be reconciled to God. Help us count the loss of this world's empty promises as great gain for the glory of Your Presence and Your purposes. Jesus, You are our exceedingly great Reward. We offer these prayers in Your powerful and glorious name. Amen.

For Discussion

1. Read Matthew 9:27–31 and Mark 8:22–26. Compare the healings recorded in those verses and jot down the differences. Why do you think Jesus healed blind eyes in different ways?

2. Read John 9:19 and compare the Pharisees' doubt about the miracle with their accusation in John 9:34. Can you pick up on the irony in the Pharisees' position? Explain.

3. Read John 9:39–41. Jesus had spoken of Himself as
   the Light of the World at the beginning of this story.
   He returns to it here in the Pharisees' hearing. Journal
   your thoughts on why Jesus uses the analogy of blind
   eyes to talk about the sin of unbelief.

CHAPTER TEN

Learn the Soul-Restoring Rhythms of Your Shepherd

D ear John,
Our Louisiana grandkids have been showing sheep at the county and state fairs for the last four or five years. It's been interesting. My husband and I were both farm kids, but neither of us participated in livestock shows growing up, so this has been all new for us. Carlisle, the middle girl, has recently decided she's done with sheep. She's into horses. Little brother Weston is looking forward to next year when he'll be old enough to show cows, and Kennedy Lee (whom you may remember from a previous chapter as KenKen the Baby Friend) is too young to choose any of the above. But Emerson, the oldest, is still all in with the sheep! In fact, she and her dad just picked up two new lambs yesterday. Frankly, John, I don't understand Emerson's affection for sheep, but I love Emerson, so I'm trying.

Last summer, my husband and I were tasked with feeding all the livestock while my son's family took a short vacation. (We farm together, so Phil and Phillip coordinate their breaks to keep the operation running.) Each evening, while Phil was involved elsewhere, yours truly was supposed to remove the lambs' face shields so they could eat. The shields are porous, allowing the lambs to drink through them while preventing them from chewing the fur off their legs. Bare legs aren't a good look come show time. Do I sound knowledgeable, John? Stay tuned.

Once the sheep were through eating, I was supposed to replace their little face shields. But the lambs didn't know me, so they refused to cooperate. I chased those silly things all over their pens, and when I finally cornered them, I'd straddle their backs and struggle to hold them still long enough to secure their masks, all while they bleated like I was killing 'em dead. This provided many a good laugh for Pops as he mucked out nearby horse stalls. Zero laughs for Keggie.

Emerson has a much easier time handling her lambs because they're hers. She feeds them regularly. She exercises them routinely. They hear her call to them daily. Sheep aren't known to be the brightest of animals, but eventually, they learn their caretaker's voice and begin to respond to it. No doubt you see where I'm going here.

I see why Jesus called us sheep! He's the Good Shepherd, willing to lead us and feed us—which would be good, great in fact, if we were wise little lambs. Smart sheep would take Him up on such an offer. Instead, we keep looking to the world around us for food and rest. We trade true fulfillment and enduring joy for the temporary fix of things we can see with our eyes and touch with our hands.

Then we wonder, privately of course, why the abundant life Jesus promised eludes us.

If only Jesus would hold us down and force us to wear shields that keep us from eating the wrong things and engaging in activities that tear at our souls. (I'm joking, John. Kinda.)

But seriously, what I've come to understand after a good long while following this Jesus is that He offers us something much better than forced fellowship. He offers the reciprocity of unforced love and the soul-restoring rhythms of divine friendship with the otherworldly One who created us and redeemed us, the Savior who made us twice His.

I see it now. He calls to us from day one, and He never stops calling, "Come! I'm the 'more' you're looking for."

I hear Him calling all the way through His Word. "Come." I've heard many a good sermon on why God gave us this privilege of choice. Can I give you my two cents? I think God made us free-will sheep because relationship is sweeter for us when we get to choose, and sweeter for the One who is chosen.

It took a lot longer than it needed to for me to realize Jesus isn't surprised by my choice-challenged nature, and He isn't berating me as I'm learning to choose Him. Far from it! He encourages us and cheers us on, right, John? He's praying for us as He bids us come. And the glorious reality is that once we decide He is what we need and head towards the sheepfold, He meets us and leads the way until we wear down a path between our life and His Door that grows sweeter with every step.

We learn to recognize Him when He speaks, and every recognition of His Voice creates in us a hunger for another. His ways become familiar as we respond. We learn what good food is by following Him. We learn refuge by resorting to Him.

It happens slowly, but it happens surely for all who keep coming, who keep spending our days in His Presence and our nights in His rest until the day comes when we realize there is nowhere else we'd rather be! And no one is more surprised than the one witnessing this change firsthand.

Bless Him. His free-will plan really is better. Isn't it, John?

Hugs,
Shellie

Dear Reader,

I truly wish I were better at remembering names. I've tried all the tricks, including associating names, rhyming names, and repeating the other person's name multiple times during our introduction. I've seen marginal improvement at best. This bothers me because I know being greeted by name makes a person feel seen and validated, and we all long to know our lives have significance. Everyone wants to matter. Sweet free-will sheep, as we read the following passage, allow yourself to consider the wonder that Jesus calls you by name.

[1] "Truly, truly I say to you, the one who does not enter by the door into the fold of the sheep, but climbs up some other way, he is a thief and a robber. [2] But the one who enters by the door is a shepherd of the sheep. [3] To him the doorkeeper opens, and the sheep listen to his voice,

and he calls his own sheep by name and leads them out."
(John 10)

Wanting to matter in itself isn't wrong, but it's a life-sucking trap if we don't know where to find true significance. The accolades and affections of other people will never meet this desire in us, and we can't satisfy it by what we achieve or accumulate. God, who calls the stars by name (Isaiah 40:26) knows you and me by ours. This is our significance. We're known by the One who created us, and He doesn't use our name lightly. He died to invite us into relationship. In the following passages Jesus begins to speak to the soul-restoring rhythms of responding to His Voice.

[4] "When he puts all his own sheep outside, he goes ahead of them, and the sheep follow him because they know his voice. [5] However, a stranger they simply will not follow, but will flee from him, because they do not know the voice of strangers." [6] Jesus told them this figure of speech, but they did not understand what the things which He was saying to them meant.

[7] So Jesus said to them again, "Truly, truly I say to you, I am the door of the sheep. [8] All those who came before Me are thieves and robbers, but the sheep did not listen to them. [9] I am the door; if anyone enters through Me, he will be saved, and will go in and out and find pasture. [10] The thief comes only to steal and kill and destroy; I came so that they would have life and have it abundantly."

How do you feel about Jesus saying we sheep know His voice? Does it resonate with your experience? Perhaps you're thinking to yourself, "But that's just it. I'm not sure I do know His voice. Does that mean I'm not His sheep?" This is a common thought that leaves many people mired in restlessness and confusion. But there can be another reason why believers don't know His Voice. We'll explore it by drilling down on verses 9 and 10.

In the first half of verse 9, Jesus says He is the door and all who enter through Him are saved. The last half tells us these reborn sheep "will go in and out and find pasture."

To "go in and out" is a biblical idiom. All cultures use idioms. They're characteristic modes of expression that can be difficult to understand outside of the culture using them. For instance, when we say it's "raining cats and dogs," we know animals aren't actually falling from the sky, but the Apostle John might look at us sideways if we said it to him.

To "go in and out" can describe a person's regular daily activities. For the children of Israel, it was a common military idiom that described leaders coming in from the battlefield to worship God, which would reinvigorate and refuel them to go back out to war in His strength and with His guidance. Those listening to Jesus describe His sheep finding pasture by "going in and out" would have understood that Jesus was talking about building a lifestyle of continual worship.

In coming in to worship Him, His sheep would be refreshed and resupplied to go out with Him, led by Him. Pasture isn't found when we check off a Bible verse, offer up a prayer, and make plans to do it again the next day while we soldier into life's demands by our brave little selves, relying on our own resources and reaching for the world's temporary fixes between our structured Jesus visits. When we do this, we cheat ourselves of all He wants to say to us between now and then.

> This is what the LORD says: "Stand at the crossroads and look; ask for the ancient paths, ask where the good way is, and walk in it, and you will find rest for your souls. But you said, 'We will not walk in it.'" (Jeremiah 6:16 NIV)

Ah, silly sheep. When will we realize that we need God's real-time, right-now Voice because life keeps invading our quiet times! The news keeps breaking and our knees keep shaking. The doctor's report comes back, and the kids forget how to act. Am I telling the truth or what? We desperately need to learn the better way, the Shepherd's ever-present way. When we hide God's written Word in our hearts and go about our daily activities with a heart of worship listening for Jesus, God's Living Word, we learn to recognize His Voice, and we get to draw from Him in the thick of it all. Jesus taught that obedient hearts give us hearing ears; obeying His Voice teaches us to recognize it. This continually resorting to Jesus builds soul-restoring rhythms into our days.

It's the abundant life Jesus the Good Shepherd offers in verse 10, and it's the birthright the thief wants to steal from us, but we don't have to let him win. Yes, our enemy works to interrupt these soul-restoring rhythms, but he loses every time we turn our spiritual eyes to Jesus and run home. Take in these next verses and then meet me below.

> ¹⁴ "I am the good shepherd; I know My sheep and My sheep know Me— ¹⁵ just as the Father knows Me and I

know the Father—and I lay down My life for the sheep.
[16] I have other sheep that are not of this sheep pen. I must
bring them also. They too will listen to My voice, and
there shall be one flock and one shepherd. . . .

[27] My sheep listen to My voice; I know them, and they
follow Me. [28] I give them eternal life, and they shall never
perish; no one will snatch them out of My hand. [29] My
Father, who has given them to Me, is greater than all; no
one can snatch them out of My Father's hand. [30] I and
the Father are one."

We are twenty-first-century sheep brought into the same fold the
first disciples enjoyed—and it's the safest of all enclosures, secured
by the Father Himself. The best life hack is found by coming in to
worship Him and going out in His refreshing strength. It's a lifestyle
we learn by intention. It's the good life we seize by design. Run home
to Jesus at the first realization that you're doing life on your own.
Run home when you're happy, run home when you're sad. Run home
when you're crushing life. Run home when life is crushing you.
Practice beating a path to God's Door, and as that path wears down,
you'll begin to discover the soul-restoring rhythms of the Shepherd.

Dear Jesus,

*Help us to find our significance in the fact that You call us by
name. Our value isn't found in physical attractiveness and talent
(or the lack of either). Remind us that we can't make our lives
matter by what we can offer this world or anything we might
accumulate in it. We want to build our lives on the value we have*

as Your dearly loved children, created and redeemed by You. We are twice Yours.

The world is growing increasingly dark, but it can't put out Your Light. We will rest there! We understand that You chose for us to be alive on Planet Earth in these days. Your Word assures us we're not here accidentally. You purposed us for this day and hour, and we can be equipped for it by listening to You. Help us live out Your plan for our lives by listening to You and sharing Truth with others.

We understand now that part of hearing Your Voice is in trusting that we do! We confess what You already know. It can be hard to believe we're hearing from You. Help us to remember that You can't lie, and You said we hear Your Voice. That tells us that when we don't think we're hearing Your Voice, it's because we have a listening problem more than a hearing problem. We commit to valuing Your Voice and listening for You so that You can train us to hear better.

And Jesus, would You alert us whenever we're trying to go it alone? We want to learn the soul-restoring rhythms of doing life with You. We want to be found running home. We ask these things in Your Precious Name. Amen.

For Discussion

1. The original language of the Old Testament was Hebrew. Type the words, "What is the Hebrew meaning of the word blessed?" into the search engine of your choice and spend some time reading the various results. Now Read Deuteronomy 28:6–7. According to your research, describe the blessings (benefits) of going in and coming out before the Lord.

2. James 1:22–25 also speaks of blessing. Read it and
   record any necessary connection you find between
   hearing God and being blessed by God.
3. Read John 10:37–38 and Romans 1:20. People often
   talk about having "blind faith" in Jesus. Do you think
   these passages support the idea that God expects us
   to have blind faith? Why or why not?

Practice Facing "What If?" with "Even Now"

D ear John,
Let's talk sports—basketball in particular. Sports are still huge here, although our spectator games aren't as bloody as the ones held at your local coliseum. Well, let me clarify that: Ours can be violent, too, but they aren't designed for executions. Big difference. But back to basketball.

Basketball is a game played by two teams with one ball. Players on the team in possession of the ball pass it around until they have an opportunity to shoot (toss) it into a basket positioned ten feet above the court to score points. While one team is trying to score on their end of the court, the opposing team is trying to take the ball away and shoot it into their own basket at the opposite end. The team to score the most points in the time allotted for the game wins. I hope my explanation didn't get lost in translation. I love basketball, John. I've played it, coached it, and I remain a big fan of the game!

As far as basketball goes, I feel like I've seen everything under the sun. Twice. I've seen my share of improbable wins and heart-breaking losses! I've seen players work together to take the ball the length of the court against a fierce defense and deliver it to a waiting teammate under their basket who should be able to score very easily. *Should.* I've seen that player miss that easy shot countless times. I've coached that player. Heck, I've been that player!

But here's what I haven't seen.

I've never witnessed a player perched atop a ladder right beside the goal being handed the ball by a teammate so he can drop it in for the win—until recently. I'm speaking analogously now, but that visual perfectly describes where I think the Church is today. In my thinking, we're the ones on the ladder. Jesus has singlehandedly decimated the defense and handed us the ball. (Stay with me, John. You're going to get this. I promise.)

For the last several years, our world has been plagued by a highly contagious virus. We had zero life experience to prepare us for living through a pandemic, but we got a crash course nonetheless, and we've been in a continuing education nightmare ever since. I suppose it could be old news by the time you read these words, but no one knows when or if this blasted virus and its mutating offspring will ever really go away. Mind you, there's no lack of opinions about that—but consensus is a scarce commodity in our time, which is why I'm just now mentioning this.

I've been wanting to talk to you about the pandemic since I first began corresponding, but the whole subject is rigged with political, emotional, and cultural land mines. I'm painfully aware some have suffered much more than others during this pandemic, so my first goal here is to do no harm. It seems impossible to work through what I want to say without my words having some sting to them, but I assure you, I'm proceeding cautiously.

Here's the gist of it: I've seen the fear of death stalking and howling its way from one end of our planet to the other. I've watched it successfully terrorize individuals and effectively paralyze towns, cities, and nations. That's understandable if this life is all a person has to live for, but a startling number of professing Christians have seemed as petrified as the unbelieving world around them. This is what grieves me, and I can't help but think it grieves Jesus.

Please don't misunderstand me. I'm no martyr, and I'm not pretending to be. I don't have a death wish, and I do realize words can be cheap until you're called to walk them out. But that's the thing, John. I can't help believing Jesus has set us believers up in this pandemic to do precisely that, to walk our faith out in a way that shows the masses of scared and searching people He loves where to find hope.

I believe Jesus overcame the enemy and He has positioned us to be conspicuously, glaringly, noticeably fearless—and then ultimately victorious, like the teammate atop the ladder. Soul-winning is His goal, and it's meant to be ours—but I'm afraid we're not scoring.

Ouch, right? Perhaps I'm being too hard on us. Maybe we are winning, here and there. But it's not enough. Far too often, the Church has looked as fearful as the faithless, and the clock is ticking.

But God.

That's one of our sayings, "But God." It means He has the last say. I'll close on that optimistic note, John, because I've also seen many a sports battle won in the closing moments, and I'm praying for the ultimate Body of Christ comeback! Talk to you soon.

> Hugs,
> Shellie

Dear Reader,

Physical death can be agonizing for the dying and crushing for those left behind. I realize both of those observations are world-class understatements.

I don't know how much loss you've experienced in the past, how recently your heart may have been broken, what prognosis you're facing, or what those you love are up against. For those reasons and many more, it'd be brutally insensitive of me to pretend death isn't painful. It would also be ignorant, especially when the Word itself speaks of death's sting (1 Corinthians 15:55). In the following passage, death has come for one of Jesus's dearest friends, and even the Savior will feel its bite.

> [1] Now a certain man was sick: Lazarus of Bethany, the village of Mary and her sister Martha. [2] And it was the Mary who anointed the Lord with ointment, and wiped His feet with her hair, whose brother Lazarus was sick. [3] So the sisters sent word to Him, saying, "Lord, behold, he whom You love is sick." [4] But when Jesus heard this, He said, "This sickness is not meant for death, but is for the glory of God, so that the Son of God may be glorified

by it." ⁵ (Now Jesus loved Martha and her sister, and Lazarus.) ⁶ So when He heard that he was sick, He then stayed two days longer in the place where He was....

¹¹ After this He said to them, "Our friend Lazarus has fallen asleep; but I am going so that I may awaken him from sleep." ¹² The disciples then said to Him, "Lord, if he has fallen asleep, he will come out of it." ¹³ Now Jesus had spoken of his death, but they thought that He was speaking about actual sleep. ¹⁴ So Jesus then said to them plainly, "Lazarus died, ¹⁵ and I am glad for your sakes that I was not there, so that you may believe; but let's go to him." (John 11)

"So that you may believe." Those are such encouraging words. Jesus is speaking to His disciples of their need to believe—even though they had already believed! But instead of reprimanding them for their ongoing need, Jesus expresses His joy in orchestrating events to reinforce their struggling faith. Death is an unavoidable fact of life. The consequential pain we feel when separated from those we love is an ongoing, in-our-face illustration of spiritual death and separation from God, and it is the goodness of God to continually put the taste and sting of it before us. Oh, what a Savior.

¹⁷ So when Jesus came, He found that he had already been in the tomb four days. ¹⁸ Now Bethany was near Jerusalem, about fifteen stadia away; ¹⁹ and many of the Jews had come to Martha and Mary, to console them about their brother. ²⁰ So then Martha, when she heard that Jesus was coming, went to meet Him, but Mary

stayed in the house. [21] Martha then said to Jesus, "Lord, if You had been here, my brother would not have died. [22] Even now I know that whatever You ask of God, God will give You."

Mark that "even now" declaration of Martha's. We'll be coming back to it.

[23] Jesus said to her, "Your brother will rise from the dead." [24] Martha said to Him, "I know that he will rise in the resurrection on the last day." [25] Jesus said to her, "I am the resurrection and the life; the one who believes in Me will live, even if he dies, [26] and everyone who lives and believes in Me will never die. Do you believe this?" [27] She said to Him, "Yes, Lord; I have come to believe that You are the Christ, the Son of God, and He who comes into the world."

It seems like Martha and Jesus are talking over each other, right? As Jesus is reminding Martha that Lazarus will never die, Martha is like, "Too little, too late, Jesus. He's already dead!" What's happening here? Is Jesus indifferent to Martha's grief? Absolutely not. We'll see proof of that as the story progresses.

Jesus sees the depth of Martha's broken heart. And while He is about to call her brother back from the grave, for now, He is fully aware it won't be the last time Martha encounters death, whether it be her own or that of someone she loves. Jesus is headed to the Cross to defeat death and make a way out of the grave for all who believe, not just Lazarus. He wants to help Martha learn to trust in this resurrection hope He has been teaching them. Jesus wants to break the tyranny of death that stalks our souls, too—and make no mistake, if it's going to happen, Jesus will have to do it. We can't.

> [28] When she had said this, she left and called Mary her sister, saying secretly, "The Teacher is here and is calling for you." [29] And when she heard this, she got up quickly and came to Him. [30] Now Jesus had not yet come into the village but was still at the place where Martha met Him. [31] Then the Jews who were with her in the house and were consoling her, when they saw that Mary had gotten up quickly and left, they followed her, thinking that she was going to the tomb to weep there. [32] So when Mary came to the place where Jesus was, she saw Him and fell at His feet, saying to Him, "Lord, if You had been here, my brother would not have died."

Mary says the same thing to Jesus that Martha had said: If He had been there, Lazarus wouldn't have died. The similarity of their responses suggests the two of them had discussed it as they waited for Jesus. And, you know what? They were right. The Word has no record of anyone ever dying in Jesus's Presence. Praise Him. And no one ever will, because Jesus is life.

> [33] Therefore when Jesus saw her weeping, and the Jews who came with her also weeping, He was deeply moved in spirit and was troubled, [34] and He said, "Where have you laid him?" They said to Him, "Lord, come and see."

[35] Jesus wept. [36] So the Jews were saying, "See how He loved him!"

Indeed, Jesus did love Lazarus. We read that earlier in the chapter. But I don't think Jesus is crying because Lazarus is dead when He knows full well He's about to see His friend again! I believe Jesus was grieving over the pain death's insidious trespass inflicts on His creation. Our Savior understands that death taunts us, but as He stands before Lazarus's tomb, He is mere days from posting an eternal victory over it.

There's absolutely nothing wrong with mourning the loss of a loved one and seeking the comfort of our Father, our friends, and our family. Grief is brutal. We would be a hardhearted lot if we didn't feel it deeply! Nor is it sinful to want to live and not die. Human history is filled with remarkable survival stories that suggest we're all born with a healthy, God-given will to survive. I'm trying to differentiate grief and the horrid sting of death from the crippling fear of dying. The two are altogether different. The fear of dying prevents us from fully living. For the believer in Christ, it is outsized dread of what could be coming that successfully obscures what is already here. The fear of dying leaves us clinging to this life, and it renders us powerless in His service.

[38] So Jesus, again being deeply moved within, came to the tomb. Now it was a cave, and a stone was lying against it. [39] Jesus said, "Remove the stone." Martha, the sister of the deceased, said to Him, "Lord, by this time there will be a stench, for he has been dead four days." [40] Jesus said to her, "Did I not say to you that if you

believe, you will see the glory of God?" ⁴¹ So they removed the stone. And Jesus raised His eyes, and said, "Father, I thank You that You have heard Me. ⁴² But I knew that You always hear Me; nevertheless, because of the people standing around I said it, so that they may believe that You sent Me." ⁴³ And when He had said these things, He cried out with a loud voice, "Lazarus, come out!" ⁴⁴ Out came the man who had died, bound hand and foot with wrappings, and his face was wrapped around with a cloth. Jesus said to them, "Unbind him, and let him go."

⁴⁵ Therefore many of the Jews who came to Mary, and saw what He had done, believed in Him. ⁴⁶ But some of them went to the Pharisees and told them the things which Jesus had done.

"Many believed." That's the glory Jesus spoke of in the early part of the narrative. Others hardened their hearts. Nothing new there. We live surrounded by the deafening noise of a culture that says the things we can see, taste, and touch is all there is or ever will be, and many of those stiff-arming Jesus are people who are dear to us. It can feel impossible to keep our own eyes fixed on Him, much less to keep praying that others will join us at His feet.

But God.

Remember how Martha said, "Even now I know that whatever you ask of God, God will give to you." Her words remind me of the "But God" phrasing I wrote about to the Apostle John. As shaky as Martha was that day, she was staking out her belief that God has the final say. We can learn a lot from her example. We can face our "what if" fears with an "even now" faith. No, God doesn't want us to cower at the threat of death, but He doesn't expect us to act like it isn't hard and we don't miss those who go before us. Because Jesus won the victory over death, we can learn to look our "what if" fears square in the face and trust that, come what may, God has us, because even now Jesus is interceding for us before the Father.

And those loved ones who are holding out against Jesus's gracious invitation? They aren't beyond His reach. Even now, we can pray for them. Even now we can see them saved. Let's quit burying people alive by deciding whose heart is too hard to yield and whose isn't, and keep believing for them and us. Even now.

Dear Jesus,

Thank You for not withdrawing from us when you see our weak faith. We praise You for the compassion You feel for our weakness. Help us remember that You never leave us because we're struggling. We praise You for not watching from a distance as we try to shore up our own faith. You understand far more than we do that we can't be strong in our faith apart from You. You're always here with us, and You're ever ready to help empower us. May we be quick to turn to You for strength and quit trying to impress You or anyone else with our own! For surely we can do nothing apart from You.

We confess our anxieties and fears. We admit to having a death grip on our physical lives that undermines our peace and wrecks our witness! Help us to seize Your eternal, abundant life in us and refuse to cling to our mortal lives, so that those who do

not believe can see our otherworldly peace and want it for themselves! We long to live fearlessly, that we might bring glory to
your Name.

Though we've come to believe that You're never far from us,
we hunger for the conscious awareness of Your Presence that
emboldens us to cry out, "Even now!" in the face of "What if?"
Would You send fresh fire? And would You forgive us for giving
up on our loved ones who have hardened their hearts against You?
We ask for a fresh anointing to pray for them and trust You for
their salvation, even now. We make these requests in Your matchless and holy name, Jesus. Amen.

For Discussion

1. The Bible study section of this chapter reminded us of
   God's kindness towards our weakness and His willing-
   ness to mature our faith. Read 2 Corinthians 12:7–10.
   Paul recognized the part he had in this holy process.
   Can you identify his discovery and journal your
   thoughts on it here?

2. Shellie contends it isn't wrong to grieve when our loved
   ones die, and it isn't sinful to want to live. Do you agree
   or disagree? Please explain your answer and then read
   Colossians 2:13–15 and 1 Corinthians 15:50–57. According to this passage, when will death quit stinging?

3. Read John 11:39 and identify Martha's complaint when
   Jesus told her to have Lazarus's tombstone removed.
   After calling Lazarus from the grave, Jesus instructed
   his mourners to remove his grave clothes. We're not told

whether those grave clothes still smelled. Do you think they did? (No wrong answer.) If the clothes did reek, what could this be telling us to expect as we help others come to Christ and follow Him? Please explain.

CHAPTER TWELVE

Value Worship over Reputation

D ear John,
I tend to be pretty enthusiastic in both my private and my public worship. I suppose some might even say "obnoxious," although I promise you, it isn't my aim to be offensive or to draw attention to myself. Worship just does that to me! On the other hand, my dear husband, the love of my life, is as quiet during worship as I am over the top. Phil is an elder at our church and he is devoted to Jesus, even if he doesn't express himself as loudly as his bride. Thankfully, however, Phil is perfectly fine with my exuberance! The man has spent many a church service worshiping God calmly and sincerely without once begrudging the stir I might be creating beside him. Am I grateful for that? You'd better believe it! In fact, it makes me want to tell you a story about Phil's longsuffering ways.

It was a typical Sunday morning, and the praise team was playing all my favorite songs. (Mind you, if Phil were in this conversation, he would laugh and add that I say this about every tune they play, and he would have a solid point.) All I can tell you is that the longer the song service lasted, the more my heart exploded in worship until it seemed like I couldn't offer God enough praise to suit me while maintaining contact with the floor. Leaning over, I jokingly whispered to Phil, "This worship is SO good! I think I'm going to need to stand on my chair!" (Note that I said "jokingly.")

We don't have pews at our church. We have individual chairs. I watched my sweetheart of forty-plus years glance at the cushioned seat behind me. Nothing in his expression changed. He didn't scowl, roll his eyes, or laugh at me. Instead, Phil whispered, "Okay, but warn me before you climb up so I can hold it steady for you."

There you go. The man never stops giving me reasons to love him, and that one definitely makes the list! I tell you this story because I hope you hear in it the freedom Phil and I give each other to worship God in our own ways, without judging the other or docking them for not doing it "our" way.

The fact is, John, I don't think loud worship is any more preferable to God than quiet adoration. Do you? And I don't believe being calm is more holy than being...well, animated. The problem, at least in our day, is that we believers can be tempted to tailor our praise to suit our peers and our surroundings. I see this as tragic on so many levels. Here's something I think applies to the conversation we've been having about how to find stable footing in a shaky world: worship is such a fiercely powerful antidote to the fear and anxiety that assails us on a daily basis.

We're bound to be uneasy, if not outright terrified, when our eyes are fixed on this earth. And if we're trying to find reassurance in our own resources, anxiety will always win. We'll never be strong enough or connected enough to insulate ourselves against this world's tribulations. Personally, I've found that merely mental acknowledgement of God in the midst of a crisis yields precious little comfort. When I'm struggling, I have to tell my soul to look up and vocalize my worship. As a matter of fact, I had to do that very thing just this morning! The Scriptures have taught me the importance of speaking right to my soul, John. Aloud. As in, "Soul, you'd better praise your God. The enemy is roaring. You'd better run for the Door that is Christ Jesus, and you best run hard!" By the way, I took that habit straight from King David,

> Bless the LORD, O my soul,
> And all that is within me, bless His holy name!
> Bless the LORD, O my soul,
> And forget not all His benefits. (Psalm 103:1–2 ESV)

That whole psalm is good stuff, but you probably know it by heart. Give David my best, will you?

The glorious thing is, once again and over and over, when I wrench my eyes from the cares of this life and turn them to Jesus, I find Him faithful.

You of all people know what I'm not saying, John. Worship doesn't always change my circumstances, but it never fails to change me, and His Presence fortifies me.

I need more of that change, and I can't get enough of Jesus because I'm a remedial learner and a work in progress—so I'm going to keep worshiping and encouraging others to do the same. And that reminds me of another church story. I'll be brief!

One Sunday morning, I was worshiping with my granddaughter Carlisle Mae perched on my hip when I belted out some encouragement to my fellow believers to, "Praise Him, church!" The thing is, that phrase was not in the lyrics, John. I didn't plan to say those words aloud, and my fellow churchgoers were already praising Him! (I bet you have a growing appreciation for my husband, don't you? I understand!) The only explanation I have is that it's like calling out to your teammates in a tense ballgame. But, back to my story.

My sweet little granddaughter pulled my neck down and stage whispered in her little-girl vernacular, "Keggie, why you say 'paise him, chuch'?"

Our family still laughs at that memory. Ask Jesus about it. I bet He enjoyed it, too!

Granted, I'm a strange one, John. But here's hoping that whatever form our worship takes, my fellow believers and I will remember that our praise encourages the faithful while holding up the glory of Jesus before the eyes of an unbelieving world. That's another win–win for the Kingdom!

Seems to me there's only one thing to say before I go: "Paise Him, chuch!"

Hugs,
Shellie

Dear Reader,

There will always be people who think our worship is a bit much and we're wasting our lives by pouring them out on Jesus.

But who's to say how many more observers will be impacted by our devotion? Take in the following story and then meet me below.

> [1] Therefore, six days before the Passover, Jesus came to Bethany where Lazarus was, whom Jesus had raised from the dead. [2] So they made Him a dinner there, and Martha was serving; and Lazarus was one of those reclining at the table with Him. [3] Mary then took a pound of very expensive perfume of pure nard and anointed the feet of Jesus and wiped His feet with her hair; and the house was filled with the fragrance of the perfume. [4] But Judas Iscariot, one of His disciples, the one who intended to betray Him, said, [5] "Why was this perfume not sold for three hundred denarii and the proceeds given to poor people?" [6] Now he said this, not because he cared about the poor, but because he was a thief, and as he kept the money box, he used to steal from what was put into it. [7] Therefore Jesus said, "Leave her alone, so that she may keep it for the day of My burial. [8] For you always have the poor with you, but you do not always have Me." (John 12)

In today's vernacular, Judas was virtue-signaling when he complained that the perfume Mary wasted on Jesus's feet could've been sold and the profits used for charity. Of course, John records Judas's true motives here, but keep in mind this was an after-the-fact observation. None of the other disciples knew Judas was stealing money from the offering when he made his big protest. It must've sounded quite noble at the time, for Mark 14:4–5 tells us some of them climbed onto Judas's moral grandstand alongside him.

Caution. Judas may have started the virtue-signaling, but those who succumbed to his fake concern and high-sounding rhetoric should give us pause. Why? Because virtue-signaling is contagious and not always easy to spot. Oh, it's easy enough to talk the popular trending talk and offer a form of worship that earns society's affirmation. Men are easily fooled. But Jesus can't be, and worship with an eye on our own reputation has zero eternal value. It yields only the temporary empty fix of this world's fickle approval.

Turning once more to Mark's account of this story, we hear Jesus speak to the lasting value of sincere worship, "Truly I say to you, wherever the gospel is preached in the entire world, what this woman has done will also be told in memory of her." Mary's worship outlived her! May this be our aim.

> [9] The large crowd of the Jews then learned that He was there; and they came, not on account of Jesus only, but so that they might also see Lazarus, whom He raised from the dead. [10] But the chief priests planned to put Lazarus to death also, [11] because on account of him many of the Jews were going away and were believing in Jesus. (John 12)

Jesus's enemies wanted Lazarus dead. Again. I'm tickled as I imagine their reasoning. *Surely if they killed Lazarus and Jesus at the same time, Lazarus would have to stay dead this time!* Little did they know Lazarus coming back to life would soon be the least of their worries! Their histrionics remind me of the old Yiddish adage, "Man plans, God laughs."

As the twelfth chapter of John continues, Jesus makes His triumphal and final entry into Jerusalem. Over the last three years,

He has become a popular figure with the masses who are gathered in the city to celebrate the Feast of Passover. Word of the many miracles He has performed has been circulating among the people, and they're primed to celebrate His arrival. As Jesus enters the city on the back of a donkey, the crowd rejoices! They throw their coats down before Him along with a mass of leafy branches in a show of allegiance and cry out together, "Praise God! Blessings on the one who comes in the name of the Lord! Hail to the King of Israel!"

Tragically, the people interpreted Jesus's entrance as His move to establish an earthly kingdom and overthrow the Romans who so long have reigned over them—a kingdom in which they would be justified, where they would finally rule. (You know, much like we want to be validated in the public square.) But it will only be a matter of hours before their expectant adoration turns to disappointment, and then to murderous rage. Their praises become demands to "crucify Him!" I hope you'll read the intervening verses for yourself, but for our purposes, I want to move to the final verses to underscore our lesson on reputation.

> [42] Nevertheless many, even of the rulers, believed in Him, but because of the Pharisees they were not confessing Him, so that they would not be excommunicated from the synagogue; [43] for they loved the approval of people rather than the approval of God.

The rulers believed Jesus was Who He claimed to be, but their belief had yet to change them and propel them to follow Him publicly because "they loved the approval of men." If we're honest, we all have a weakness for the tonic of praise. Believers aren't immune.

We can even break free of our addiction to the world's approval only to trade it for the applause of other believers. Heaven help us, amen? Amen, indeed! Only God can break the power of the siren song of others' affirmation and approval.

Apart from God, we're like street musicians, spending our lives performing for onlookers, waiting for them to drop their little tokens of approval in our awaiting cups. With God, our desires can change and our values be reordered, and it all happens in His Presence. Worship transforms us. Praise Him with me!

Dear Jesus,

You are all-glorious. We give You our praise and adoration. Help us. We long to keep Your glory as our aim, to be as indifferent to other people's opinions of us as Mary was when she poured that costly perfume on Your precious feet and wiped them with her hair. We acknowledge that, should our praise incur the disapproval of any other human, it is a most inconsequential loss! You tell us in the Word that Your thoughts of us are more numerous than the grains of sand that line our oceans (Psalm 139:17–18). Teach us to thrill to this, to Your thoughts of us, and free us from the trap of self-consciousness that makes us concerned with what other people think. You alone bore our sin debt. You alone reconciled us to Your Father and ours. You alone are worthy of praise.

Jesus, we confess that we can stand among men and offer worship to You with our lips even when our hearts are cold and hard. This grieves us. Save us from sham praise. We don't want to be virtue-signalers. We long to be authentic worshipers. Oh, how we need You! Unite our hearts, minds, and souls in sincere adoration for all You have done, for all You are.

And Lord, help us not trade the approval of unbelievers for the applause of the church. Cause our praise to ring with an authenticity that reverberates in our families, our communities, and our world, leading many to turn to You for salvation. Teach us to give you the glory You deserve. In Your precious name we pray, Jesus. Amen.

For Discussion

1. Historians say the perfume Mary poured on Jesus's feet was likely a treasure that had been in her family for some time. Read John 12:7 and then Mark 16:1. What was Mary on her way to do in the latter passage? Do you see any significance between that moment and this one in the Gospel of John? What does Jesus allowing Mary's act of devotion tell you about Him? Please elaborate.

2. Read Zechariah 9:9, Matthew 3:11, John 14:6, and Acts 2:3. John tells us the disciples didn't immediately recognize that Jesus was fulfilling Scripture when He rode into Jerusalem on a donkey. What does this tell you about why they were able to make the connection after He was taken into glory, but not before?

3. Read John 12:22–31. What purpose do you think Jesus had in mind when He said the voice that spoke from Heaven was not for His sake, but for the people's? If you're not sure, consider 2 Peter 3:8–9. What adjectives are used to describe God in this passage?

CHAPTER THIRTEEN

Choose Down as the Way Up

D ear John,
   Just between us, that Peter is something else. Do tell, is he still as impulsive as ever, only in a fully sanctified way? I don't know what that would look like, but I'm curious, because I get Peter. I have a jump-first, ask-questions-later mentality, too, and I've been known to speak when silence would better serve. I've run across a few places in Scripture that record Peter saying something inappropriate for the moment because "he didn't know what else to say." I resemble that. Got myself a growing collection of those foot-in-mouth blunders.

So, yes, I'm sure my spur-of-the-moment reaction when Jesus suddenly started washing feet would've been much like Peter's. I would've been super quick to voice my objections. And there's no doubt about it: had Jesus responded by telling me that washing my feet was a requirement if I were going to belong to Him, I would've turned on a dime and asked for a full-body bathing, too, just like dear old Peter.

Are you wondering why I'm so sure of this? I can explain. As I sit here writing to you, I understand the point Jesus was driving home to Peter that evening. I know Jesus washes us from the penalty of sin when we come to believe in Him—but we all sin again as we follow Him, which requires ongoing cleansing. I also know it's not necessary or possible to get "saved" again! Amen? It's impossible to pass back and forth repeatedly between life and death. At least, I know all these things intellectually because it's taught throughout the Scriptures. But, oh, John. Let me just tell you. Head knowledge alone has failed me more times than I can count. Allow me to describe the snare that always seems to be waiting for my feet.

If I hear that I'm supposed to do *A* to walk with Jesus (let Him wash my feet), I'm susceptible to doubling down and trying to check off *A* (dunk me again, Jesus!) like it's my ticket to glory. *Look at me, Lord. I'm following all the requirements and then some!*

I hope you understand that I'm not denying or discounting the importance of obedience. As you know, it's all over the Scriptures. You wrote plenty on it yourself, and I'm looking forward to discussing more on that subject with you in coming letters. But to my current point, without the Holy Spirit's real-time help, I can get crossways in my desire to be obedient. I wrote extensively about this in a book called *Finding Deep and Wide*, but since you haven't had an opportunity to read it, I'll sum it up here.

When I fail to offer God a spotless obedience record (and I always fail), I often find myself trying to work my way back into His favor—as if what I had been doing or not doing up to that point had been gaining me access to His sweet friendship and the soul peace I find there, instead of the spotless blood of Christ and His finished work. I know. I'll say it, and you won't have to: "Heaven, forbid!"

Honestly, John, I know that type of works mentality is twisted theology! I'm well aware that my self-will and determined efforts are powerless. And yet, the only way I've learned to avoid that legalistic snare is by keeping my eyes fixed on Jesus and asking Him to alert me when it's tightening around my feet! I'm forever grateful for His faithfulness to remind me to keep preaching the Gospel to myself and to keep running for the Light.

One more thing before I close. I wasn't picking on Peter. I'm grateful for his example. Tell the old fisherman this opinionated twenty-first-century believer has learned a lot from him. I watched him learn how to temper his impulsive nature and minister the Gospel in humility while still being passionate about Jesus. Have mercy. There's hope for me yet!

Hugs,
Shellie

Dear Reader,

Bible history tells us the following story took place on Holy Thursday, the day before Jesus's crucifixion. Holy Thursday is also known as Maundy Thursday. The word "maundy" comes from "mandate." It's a reference to the new commandment Jesus gave His followers to love one another as He loved them. It was during the Last Supper on Maundy Thursday that Jesus, the greatest show-and-tell Teacher ever, illustrated His new commandment with a startling and unexpected display of humility.

¹ Now before the Feast of the Passover, Jesus, knowing that His hour had come that He would depart from this world to the Father, having loved His own who were in the world, He loved them to the end. ² And during supper, the devil having already put into the heart of Judas Iscariot, the son of Simon, to betray Him, ³ Jesus, knowing that the Father had handed all things over to Him, and that He had come forth from God and was going back to God, ⁴ got up from supper and laid His outer garments aside; and He took a towel and tied it around Himself.

⁵ Then He poured water into the basin and began washing the disciples' feet and wiping them with the towel which He had tied around Himself. ⁶ So He came to Simon Peter. He said to Him, "Lord, You are washing my feet?" ⁷ Jesus answered and said to him, "What I am doing, you do not realize right now, but you will understand later." ⁸ Peter said to Him, "Never shall You wash my feet!" Jesus answered him, "If I do not wash you, you have no place with Me." ⁹ Simon Peter said to Him, "Lord, then wash not only my feet, but also my hands and my head!" ¹⁰ Jesus said to him, "He who has bathed needs only to wash his feet; otherwise he is completely clean. And you are clean—but not all of you." (John 13)

John opens this account by describing Jesus's mindset, and it's fascinating information. We learn that Jesus knew His hour had come, but He wasn't thinking about Himself. Amazingly, His heart and mind were filled with love for His disciples instead of concern for what lay ahead for Himself. Can we put ourselves in those holy shoes for a moment? What would you say to your closest family and friends if you knew you were about to die? I don't know exactly what I'd choose to do with my last moments on Earth, but I'm certain I wouldn't waste time! I'd want to share only the most important things I wanted them to remember. This is where we find Jesus—and His "most important thing" is to impress on His loved ones that the way up is down. The Romans derided humility and the Greeks despised the common labor of servants; Jesus illustrates both.

Jesus, secure in His identity, feels no compulsion to protect His status in the disciples' eyes. How telling is that witness! How foreign to our world. It's worth reminding ourselves of His example whenever we're feeling slighted, unappreciated, or unimportant. Clamoring for position and influence, needing recognition or approval—these are tell-tale signs that we aren't looking to Jesus for our identity. It should alert us that we've let ourselves become sidetracked and subsequently forgotten who we are.

Sometimes I need refresher courses on this truth, but it's mostly just on days that end in "y." Thankfully, Jesus has convinced me of the futility of chastising myself when I realize I've slipped into the gaping pit of self and her many wants and needs, be they material or emotional. It's impossible to sever this world's pull on our souls apart from God's help. He is the Only One who can reorder our values.

One of the many privileges of our new birth is being able to run to Him and ask Him to forgive us, heal our thinking, and change our perspective. I've found that He delights to help, and in His light, my need to protect or defend myself fades and my desire to point others to Him grows stronger.

That rather unattractive bit of bio is an example of the principle of continual cleansing Jesus was unpacking for Peter. Jesus explained that Peter didn't need a full bath. It was only his feet that needed washing because they had come in contact with Israel's roadways. Likewise, when you and I put our trust in Jesus, He gives us new life and washes us clean from the penalty of sin. And yet, just like Peter's feet, our souls will need ongoing cleansing while we walk this dusty planet. The Bible calls this process "sanctification," and Jesus provides it as we do life with Him in His Word. Let's read on as Jesus continues to unpack His lesson on living upside-down from the world's ways.

> [12] Then, when He had washed their feet, and taken His garments and reclined at the table again, He said to them, "Do you know what I have done for you? [13] You call Me 'Teacher' and 'Lord'; and you are correct, for so I am. [14] So if I, the Lord and the Teacher, washed your feet, you also ought to wash one another's feet. [15] For I gave you an example, so that you also would do just as I did for you. [16] Truly, truly I say to you, a slave is not greater than his master, nor is one who is sent greater than the one who sent him. [17] If you know these things, you are blessed if you do them."

Knowing His hours on Earth were soon ending, Jesus wasn't content with merely instructing the disciples not to think too highly of themselves. He wanted to impress on them the importance of actually doing it, of practicing humility and tending to one another's needs. To show them what that would look like, He took water and a towel and proved that He, their Teacher and Lord, did not consider caring for their dirty feet to be beneath Him. Having secured their attention, He called them to follow His example.

Jesus's show-and-tell lesson couldn't be further from the mantra of our day. Society says, "Save yourself. Promote yourself. Defend yourself. Tend to yourself!" Jesus challenges us to crucify self and believe that the peace and joy we're chasing can be ours by resisting the endless competition, self-promotion, and self-interest of our culture to do life His way—to die to self over and again.

Will it be easy to live out this teaching, to believe that down is the way up? No. Will it be worth it? Yes! A thousand times, yes. To encourage such down-is-the-way-up living, Jesus holds out a promise: while simply knowing such truth won't change us, blessing awaits the one who practices it. We'll read Jesus's glorious new commandment to love like He loves in the following verses. I'll meet you below them for some closing thoughts on the blessing of living to acknowledge God and love others instead of living to be acknowledged and loved by others.

> [33] "Little children, I am still with you a little longer. You will look for Me; and just as I said to the Jews, now I also say to you: 'Where I am going, you cannot come.' [34] I am giving you a new commandment, that you love one another; just as I have loved you, that you also love one another. [35] By this all people will know that you are My disciples: if you have love for one another."

Let's be stone-cold honest: Loving others the way Jesus loves us gets a whole lot harder when the ones we're loving don't seem to be recognizing our efforts or reciprocating. Worse yet, there's the hit our hearts take when their response to our gestures is yet another insult or offense. Ugh. Right? Feeling unappreciated or overlooked stings, and not getting the affection and attention we want or think we need hurts. Maybe that's why Jesus reminded us of the blessing found in heeding His teaching. Perhaps it's His way of encouraging us that regardless of how we're received, it's in our best interest to love big anyway!

Can I testify to that promised blessing with some personal experience? I once tried to wrangle the type of ugly feelings I mentioned above into submission by reminding myself that God loved me, God saw me, God valued me, etc. This is true, and that practice is good. If you're doing it, don't stop! But in the last few years, I've learned an additional, deeper way of dealing with those situations that has yielded even greater blessing!

If I feel unappreciated by someone, I commit to continuing to show love to the person who isn't responding the way I might want. Then I go a step further. I turn my mind to God, and I begin voicing my appreciation to Him for any and every blessing I can think to list. Likewise, if I'm feeling overlooked or slighted, I reassure myself of my value in my Father's eyes, but I don't camp there. Instead, I remind myself to begin valuing and praising Who He Is! Are you seeing the pattern? Instead of trying to get God to fill my tank without whatever it is I think I need from another person, I flip that need into the form of a praise!

We can practice this with our desires for appreciation, affection, affirmation, acclamation, or acknowledgment. (Alliteration is a powerful memory tool!) This sort of holy swap never fails to turn ugliness on its head, cancel the monopoly of torturous thoughts, and soothe what's troubling me. That is, if I can wrench my eyes off of poor me and put them on Holy Him!

I said "if" because the reality is we're always dwelling with our problems—or dwelling with the Problem Solver. Every opportunity for offense comes with the choice to pet it or release it. We can dwell with what is irritating, frustrating, or painful, or we can dwell with Jesus. The ugliness we cling to holds a hidden but blessed road that can carry us to Jesus to be corrected, instructed, and comforted.

Sometimes I remember this more quickly than other times. Sometimes I remember, but I'd prefer to dwell with the ugly—even though I know The Way out! That's so twisted. But you know exactly what I'm describing, don't you? You've been there, too, haven't you? Maybe you're there right now.

So, how do we reach when we'd rather resent? By flat-out confessing our inability to let go of the ugly and asking Jesus to help us choose the better way. When we choose Him, we find Him faithful—and the more we choose Him, the easier it becomes, until we make one forevermore life-changing discovery. The love we owe others is our due obedience, but the blessing that rebounds is every bit ours, because it's nothing less than His abiding Presence, and He is eternally worth it!

Dear Jesus,

Help! We want to learn the power of Your new commandment. We want to love others the way You love us. Thank you for stepping down from Heaven to live and die for sinful, self-seeking us, and then taking Your life back up again, all to reconcile us to the Father. Your sacrificial life demonstrated what it looks like to prefer others over ourselves, and now You intercede for us so we might learn Your ways. Forgive us for the sin of choosing ourselves, and dwelling so often with our pet wounds when we have the precious gift of Your Spirit dwelling with us to empower us to follow Your example.

Thank you for the gift of our salvation. You are eternal Life, living in us. We thank You for washing us in Your own dear blood and freeing us from sin's dreadful curse. Help us resist the enemy and walk in obedience to You. But when the filth of this world dirties our souls as we follow You home, remind us of our great privilege of coming to You for cleansing.

We want to give grace to those who hurt us and forgiveness those who offend us, just as You have graced us and forgiven us. Help us be ever mindful of Your willingness to support us when we intentionally choose Your ways, that we might dwell in Your Presence. For You, Jesus, are our ulterior motive! The good life is found in Your Presence. Amen.

For Discussion

1. Jesus knew who He was. He understood His mission and He knew the hour of His departure had come. Read Luke 22:27, Galatians 4:7, and Romans 8:28. Our world has much to say about how we identify ourselves. Take some time to explain what it means to you to identify as a follower of Christ.

2. Read Hebrews 6:4–6 and John 13:11. Considering our discussion and the fact that Jesus said all the

disciples were not clean, though He had just washed their feet, what do you think this passage suggests about Judas?

3. Read John 13:19. Sit a moment with the understanding that Jesus said He was telling His most intimate friends about things to come to help them believe. Describe what that does for you.

CHAPTER FOURTEEN

Listen for the Spirit and Follow Him Home

Dear John,

Do people still dream in Heaven? (I realize that's a strange opener, but I figure you're getting used to me by now.) Though I suppose the better question would be, do people still *sleep* in Heaven? It's my understanding we'll have perfected bodies, so we probably won't require sleep, but I think I'll miss naps. I don't take them that often, but on the occasional Sunday afternoon when I do allow myself a little siesta on the couch with the sun warming my bones through the living room window, it can feel like...well, Heaven. Or our idea of it. You remember how it is, don't you, John? We don't know what we don't know.

I ask about dreams because I've been having versions of a recurring dream for years now. While I can see myself missing naps, I'd gladly give up the nighttime dramas I've taken to calling my "searching dreams." They come like clockwork, and I always wake up from them feeling totally drained and depleted. It's almost impossible to explain them to a second party, but if you'll bear with me, I want to try.

My searching dreams always have a destination I urgently need to reach—only I'm unable to make any forward progress because the settings and the circumstances keep changing. I may start out on a bike that morphs into a car, or a motorcycle that becomes a boat, or a plane that becomes a tractor, but whatever vehicle I'm traveling in will inevitably fail and force me to change modes of transportation around the time the road loops back, detours, or washes out completely, leaving me to find yet another game plan as my destination lies tantalizingly near, yet so far out of reach. These different but similar scenarios loop throughout the dream, which may be minutes or even seconds long, but it feels like hours. Bottom line: I'm always trying to get somewhere I desperately need to be, and yet I never have a way to call my family and friends or communicate that I'm in trouble.

Anxiety, pressure, fear, and stress—these are the unwelcome climates of my searching dreams. As you might imagine, they wear me out. I used to ask God to take them away, but I don't anymore.

Some time ago, after another long night of getting nowhere fast and waking up sweaty and exhausted, I decided that instead of asking God to stop the dreams, I'd ask Him for understanding concerning them. We have qualified psychologists down here who would love to take a stab at the workings of my brain, but I want to tell you what I've come to believe.

I think Father God allows me to feel all the frustration, anxiety, fear, and exhaustion during the night that others feel in the daytime when they're wide awake and searching for meaning and satisfaction in this world apart from a relationship with Jesus. I believe it's all so my heart might be burdened to pray for and minister to theirs. It's why I've quit asking Him to take the dreams away. I'm convinced that whatever people think they're searching for, what they need is Jesus—and to whatever degree these dreams help me share the good news of Jesus with this world, it's worth it. Losing a little sleep pales in significance to the Light of the One who gave us His life.

Not long ago, I was having yet another searching dream when the plot took a crazy turn, even for me. The dream began pretty much like all the ones that have come before it: I couldn't get anywhere. I couldn't make any progress, and I was miles from anyone or anything familiar. I was also on foot in a train tunnel of sorts, having long since lost transportation of any kind. To make the situation even more dire, I couldn't move, and the walls were swaying and crumbling around me. I was a goner.

With danger surrounding me and uncertainty overwhelming me, my beloved husband suddenly appeared at my side. I stood rooted to the ground, incredulous that he had managed to find me.

"What are you doing here?" I whispered.

Phil reached out and took my trembling hand in his. "Let's go," he said. "I came to take you home."

That's where the dream ended, John, but I can recall the peace that enveloped me with his words. I've since found my thoughts returning to that sweet scene over and again. For a long time after that, the searching dreams stopped, and I decided that last tunnel disaster and subsequent rescue had been the finale. It felt right. It made sense. But then the dreams returned.

That's okay, too. I have one more piece of the story now. We humans love a good drama, and that tunnel dream encourages me to keep sharing the good news of the grandest rescue ever. I love to tell people that one day, many years ago, our Hero stepped into the middle of our sin-wrecked world. Amen? And I'm crazy fond of how Paul said it in Ephesians...

> Remember that you were at that time separate from Christ, excluded from the people of Israel, and strangers to the covenants of the promise, having no hope and without God in the world. (Ephesians 2:12)

We were all stranded here on Planet Earth without God, lost and alone and without hope, when Jesus showed up, reached for us, and whispered words of love: "I came to take you home."

John, I aim to tell that story on this side of Heaven until I meet you on that one. And I intend to keep reminding anyone who'll listen that we can let our sore, tired hearts hold onto His unfailing love without hesitation, because this great rescue is final. Finished. Done. See you soon, John.

Hugs,
Shellie

Dear Reader,

After Jesus washed the disciples' feet in John 13, He shared a meal with them known to us as the Last Supper. During supper, Jesus announced that one of them was about to betray Him, and that betrayal would be followed by His death and departure from their midst. While it wasn't the first time Jesus had prophesied of His death, and they had never really understood what He meant, He was now saying the time had come. Can you picture their faces as they tried to process what they were hearing? Jesus undoubtedly saw it, for He spoke directly into their confusion and anguish in the famous words of our next passage. They are some of the dearest words to me in all the Word. Listen as Jesus soothes His friends. It's true. Soon they will be unable to see Him physically, but Jesus promises to come back for them. And as the narrative continues, Jesus reveals that He will be just as near to them after His death as He has been before it. Grab these words and hold them close. They're our Living Hope, too!

> [1] "Do not let your heart be troubled; believe in God, believe also in Me. [2] In My Father's house are many rooms; if that were not so, I would have told you, because I am going there to prepare a place for you. [3] And if I go and prepare a place for you, I am coming again and will take you to Myself, so that where I am, there you also will be. [4] And you know the way where I am going."
> [5] Thomas said to Him, "Lord, we do not know where You are going; how do we know the way?" [6] Jesus said to him, "I am the way, and the truth, and the life; no one comes to the Father except through Me. [7] If you had known Me, you would have known My Father also; from now on you know Him, and have seen Him." (John 14)

Sounds like Thomas voiced what everyone else was thinking. How were they supposed to follow Him when they didn't know where He was going? It would seem the disciples found Jesus's patient explanation that He was the Way to the Father equally mysterious and unsatisfying. I can almost see Thomas tagging Philip. *You're up, brother.*

> [8] Philip said to Him, "Lord, show us the Father, and it is enough for us." [9] Jesus said to him, "Have I been with you for so long a time, and yet you have not come to know Me, Philip? The one who has seen Me has seen the Father; how can you say, 'Show us the Father'? [10] Do you not believe that I am in the Father, and the Father is in Me? The words that I say to you I do not speak on My own, but the Father, as He remains in Me, does His works. [11] Believe Me that I am in the Father and the Father is in Me; otherwise believe because of the works themselves."

Philip asked for a sign, as if the moment called for yet another of Jesus's miracles they could see with their natural eyes. I mean, surely that would help. Right? Or would they need another, and then another?

Jesus asked the disciples to believe that something far greater than a one-time supernatural event was available to them. He lays the same opportunity before us today. Supernatural, eternal life begins now for all who will embrace Jesus as the manifestation of the unseen God, trust Him right where we are, and listen for His next instruction in the very midst of all our worldly uncertainty. Jesus said His works validated these words.

Believe in God, He said, *believe also in Me.*

The hope that steadies our troubled hearts is found in trusting that the great God out there is right here, and listening for His indwelling Spirit as we read His Word and come to Him in prayer. It's the Promise of the Helper, the indwelling God, the Way alive within us.

Jesus was leaving, but He assured His disciples, and He assures us, that Holy Spirit would come to live this life with us and lead us home. He is present when all feels right, and also when the wheels have fallen off and the tunnel walls are closing in around us.

> [16] "I will ask the Father, and He will give you another Helper, so that He may be with you forever; [17] the Helper is the Spirit of truth, whom the world cannot receive, because it does not see Him or know Him; but you know Him because He remains with you and will be in you. [18] I will not leave you as orphans; I am coming to you. [19] After a little while, the world no longer is going to see Me, but you are going to see Me; because I live, you also will live. [20] On that day you will know that I am in My Father, and you are in Me, and I in you. [21] The one who has My commandments and keeps them is the one who loves Me; and the one who loves Me will be loved by My Father, and I will love him and will reveal Myself to him."

You and I sit with the disciples as we read those words. Their challenge is ours. Will we believe and embrace the life Jesus spelled out for them, the one He is holding out for us? Revealed with beautiful simplicity, Jesus says He isn't leaving them to fight the battle alone, and we aren't left here as twenty-first-century orphans, either. Jesus has come back to live with us through His Holy Spirit, and He is willing to reveal Himself to believers in ways the world around us will never see.

Jesus literally made a way for us to live with God. Can we quit asking for one more sign or signal and set our hearts to trust and obey Him? We won't be able to do this through our own determined efforts, but Jesus is more than willing to form this way of life in us. Will we ask Him to teach us how to lean on the Helper and draw strength and nourishment from the Spirit? If so, we'll discover His indwelling Spirit is more than enough for today's troubles and tomorrow's uncertainties.

Jesus speaks again of obeying Him and abiding in Him in the closing words of this scene and in the next chapter. We'll talk about obedience in the next chapter. For now, let's read a bit more of this one. There's something I want to celebrate with you.

> [22] Judas (not Iscariot) said to Him, "Lord, what has happened that You are going to reveal Yourself to us and not to the world?" [23] Jesus answered and said to him, "If anyone loves Me, he will follow My word; and My Father will love him, and We will come to him and make Our dwelling with him. [24] The one who does not love Me does not follow My words; and the word which you hear is not Mine, but the Father's who sent Me. [25] These things I have spoken to you while remaining with you. [26] But the Helper, the Holy Spirit whom the Father will send in My name, He will teach you all things, and remind you of all that I said to you. [27] Peace I leave you, My peace I give you; not as the world gives, do I give to

you. Do not let your hearts be troubled, nor fearful.
28 You heard that I said to you, 'I am going away, and I
am coming to you.' If you loved Me, you would have
rejoiced because I am going to the Father, for the Father
is greater than I."

Our scene ends much as it began, with Jesus promising peace
the world can't deliver and reiterating His earlier message. He is
indeed leaving in His physical form, but the disciples don't have to
be troubled or fearful, because His death and resurrection means
all believers will have full-time, any-time access to God the Father
through God the Spirit because of the sacrificial death of God the
Son.

As believers reconciled to God, we are at home with God in the
Spirit now. And He, the Spirit of God, is our ever-ready guide here
to lead us to our forever Home—one step, one instruction, at a
time.

Holy Spirit is a most patient Teacher. He guides all who choose
to follow, and He picks us up when we stumble instead of con-
demning us for tripping. That's soul-steadying stuff. But the last
sentence—it's icing on the cake.

29 "And now I have told you before it happens, so that
when it happens, you may believe."

There's our Jesus, once again telling His closest friends, who
already believe, things that will help them continue to believe. It's
okay if you aren't shouting. I needed to hear that, and I'm loud
enough for both of us!

Dear Jesus,

*Thank You for caring so much for our fretful human hearts.
Sadly, we have little trouble believing that You're done with us
when we're worried and anxious. Our doubts embarrass us and
leave us open to the enemy's accusations that we have failed You
again. It's harder for us to accept that Your response to our
troubled souls is to speak peace to them, and yet the evidence is
right here in Your Word. Your heart is turned to ours when we're
in turmoil. Remind us, Lord. Help us run to You with our concerns instead of hiding from You in shame or pretending our
souls are well when they aren't. Both reactions cheat us of the
opportunity to know You more and be strengthened in Your
Presence.*

*Jesus, we confess that we're as guilty as the disciples ever were
of wanting to see physical proof that You're with us. It's ugly, but
it's true. We can spend our whole lives wanting to see You solve
our problems more than we want to see You, the Problem Solver.
Forgive us. Heal us. Circumcise our hearts to love You with a
greater zeal. Give us an increasing passion to know You intimately,
even as we are known by You.*

*Thank You for inspiring John to record so many instances that
testify of Your divine intention to help us believers keep believing.
It's beyond encouraging to know You're partnering with us as we
seek to grow in faith. Thank you for not grading us from a distance, Jesus. Thank you for living in us to reveal Yourself to us and
complete what You've begun in us. It's in Your sweet name that
we rest and pray. Amen.*

For Discussion

1. Read John 14:2–3. Jesus says He's leaving to prepare a place for the disciples, and He will return for them. Do you think Jesus is talking about the dwelling place He is preparing for them (and us!) in Heaven and His second coming? Or could Jesus be referring to the work He's about to do on the Cross that will prepare a meeting place between God and man, and His subsequent return through the coming of Holy Spirit? Could both be true? Take a moment to explain your answer.

2. Read John 14:15–19, 14:22–23, and 19:30, and Hebrews 1:1–3. Now, review your answer to the first question. Do these verses help to confirm your earlier response, or do they change it? Explain.

3. Read Hebrews 6:19–20. This verse calls Jesus our "forerunner." Look up the definition of forerunner and record it here. Jesus finished the work of salvation, but He is very much actively involved in our faith today. Read Romans 8:34. Describe Jesus's ongoing work on our behalf and any response or commitment it moves you to make.

CHAPTER FIFTEEN

Discover the Power of Abiding

D ear John,
     I've never been good at sitting still. I hope that won't be a problem in Heaven. My family called me Wiggle Worm when I was a kid. I didn't like the name, but it fit like a glove. My fidgeting led to countless accidents, especially at meals, where I'd usually spill my drink despite my best intentions. It became so common my Papa took to saying things like, "Shellie, go ahead and spill your milk now so your Mama can clean it up before we eat." I wasn't a fan of that little routine, even though I knew Papa was joking with me.

Honestly, I kind of assumed being still would get easier as I got older. That hasn't happened. Granted, I'm much better at not fidgeting outwardly. My problem is more mental. (And if you didn't crack a joke there, John, you are totally nicer than anyone in my circle of family and friends!) To clarify, my mind is always going a hundred miles an hour, and if there's an off switch, I wish someone would tell me where to find it.

I've always loved the calming words of Psalm 46:10, "Be still and know that I am God," but they used to make me feel like one big failure. I'd try to be still and think about God, but my mind would race off to think about, well, anything and everything else. Like baby elephants! Did you know baby elephants aren't born with the ability to control their trunks? They have to learn that motor skill. I saw the cutest video of a baby elephant trying to wrangle his slap-happy trunk into submission long enough to get a sip of water. Bless him. And me. Bless me, for I've digressed again. But now you see what I'm dealing with, don't you, John?

It's okay to laugh at me, or with me. These days I'm totally okay with the way God wired me. And it's all because the One who inspired the Psalmist to record those soothing words is teaching me how to live in Him, and it's producing a relationship with Jesus I dreamed of but never thought I'd be able to experience.

For instance, I'm learning I don't have to let my runaway brain frustrate me and cause me to give up when I'm trying to pray. As soon as I realize I'm thinking about baby elephants (or whatever else has captured my attention), I simply bring my wandering thoughts back and put them back on Jesus as many times as necessary without allowing myself to get bogged down in guilt or shame. This simple lesson is helping me stay in God's Presence longer, and His Presence is helping me love prayer all the more. It's a glorious cycle, and there's more. I'm learning (emphasis on learning) not to walk out of prayer once I leave my dedicated devotional time, but to walk in prayer, keeping the line of communication open and ongoing. This is allowing me to experience the same principle of returning for rest, guidance, and fresh nourishment from Jesus all through the day, even when I'm in nonstop motion! Praise Him.

I realize I'm not telling you anything new, John. I just wanted to celebrate together and thank you for recording Jesus's teachings on the power of abiding in Him. I'm definitely a work in progress, but this Wiggle Worm is deeply grateful to be sharing the journey with Jesus. He is everything. See you soon!

Hugs,
Shellie

Dear Reader,

Your Bible translation might use the word "abide" in the following passages, where the one I've chosen (NASB) uses "remain." I think both words are valuable in helping us grasp this precious instruction to stay close to Jesus and do life with Him after we come to faith. Here are a few definitions of what it means to remain: "To go on being. To endure or persist. To continue in the same place, state, or condition. To be left after removal, loss, or passage. To stay behind after others have gone." We're going to squeeze the goodness out of those definitions as we take in the following passage by inserting them in parentheses.

[1] "I am the true vine, and My Father is the vinedresser. [2] Every branch in Me that does not bear fruit, He takes away; and every branch that bears fruit, He prunes it so that it may bear more fruit. [3] You are already clean because of the word which I have spoken to you. [4] Remain in Me, (go on being, endure, persist, continue

in the same place, state, or condition, be left after removal, loss, or passage, stay behind after others have gone) in Me, and I in you. Just as the branch cannot bear fruit of itself but must remain in the vine, so neither can you unless you remain in Me." (John 15)

Did you get stuck at the mention of pruning? I understand. We wouldn't be the first believers to think that perhaps we don't want to bear fruit if it's going to lead to more pruning. But then, verse 2 says the fruitless branch gets taken away. What? We'll unpack that shortly. For now, take comfort in this thought: The Vinedresser is ever so close when He is pruning His kids. You can't prune from a distance. Pruning is a hands-on process, and our God is compassionate and trustworthy.

Besides, I believe we confuse pruning with discipline, and pruning is sweeter than we imagine for those who remain in Jesus. Why? Because He promises that when we remain in Him, He will remain in us (go on being, endure, persist, continue in the same place, state, or condition, be left after removal, loss, or passage, stay behind after others have gone). Bottom line, Jesus is with us for the duration.

The literal word for pruning in John 15:2 is "cleaning," which is what happens when a gardener removes things from the vine that are negatively affecting its growth. Note that Jesus goes on to tell the disciples in the next verse that they're already clean before explaining that if they abide in Him, they'll bear fruit and receive further pruning (cleansing). Lean in here. This is good news. We think pruning always involves cutting, but when we remain close to Jesus, the further pruning can sometimes be more akin to washing, and it doesn't always have to be painful. I'll show you.

In John 17:17, Jesus is praying to the Father about those who have believed in Him when He makes the following request: *Sanctify them in the truth. Your Word is truth.*

The word "sanctify" means to bless, consecrate, cleanse, purify, and make holy. And Jesus says it happens through the truth of God's Word. I believe our choices play a part in the pruning process. It's to our benefit to allow the Word of God to have full reign in our lives by choosing to remain in Jesus. We can learn from Scripture, listen for the guiding voice of Holy Spirit, and heed divine correction as it comes to us, or we can refuse to abide in Him and endure the painful, disciplining side of pruning.

Years ago, I told my kids they didn't have to learn everything the hard way! They could be the people who didn't have to touch the stove to believe it was hot. They could abide by my instruction and save themselves a painful experience. Please hear me out. I'm not saying that by remaining in Jesus we can expect to escape all hardship. Jesus Himself promised us trouble in this life.

"In the world you will have tribulation. But take heart;
I have overcome the world." (John 16:33 ESV)

What I am saying is that by choosing to remain in Jesus (go on being, endure, persist, continue in the same place, state, or condition, be left after removal, loss, or passage, stay behind after others have gone), much of our pruning can come through the Word because the Word will cleanse our lives of many of the things negatively affecting our fruit-bearing.

As much as I love the sound of that, I'm not wearing rose-colored glasses as I write these words. You and I would be naïve (if not deceived!) to think we won't ever need discipline. But when it comes, Scripture encourages us that we can reap its benefits by remaining in Jesus. We find this principle again in Hebrews 12:4–11:

> You have not yet resisted to the point of shedding blood in your striving against sin; and you have forgotten the exhortation, which is addressed to you as sons,
>
> "MY SON, DO NOT REGARD LIGHTLY THE DISCIPLINE OF THE LORD, NOR FAINT WHEN YOU ARE PUNISHED BY HIM; FOR WHOM THE LORD LOVES HE DISCIPLINES, AND HE PUNISHES EVERY SON WHOM HE ACCEPTS."
>
> It is for discipline that you endure; God deals with you as with sons; for what son is there whom his father does not discipline? But if you are without discipline, of which all have become partakers, then you are illegitimate children and not sons. Furthermore, we had earthly fathers to discipline us, and we respected them; shall we not much more be subject to the Father of spirits, and live? For they disciplined us for a short time as seemed best to them, but He disciplines us for our good, so that we may share His holiness. For the moment, all discipline seems not to be pleasant, but painful; yet to those who have been trained by it, afterward it yields the peaceful fruit of righteousness.

When it comes, discipline isn't pleasant, but understanding its fruit-bearing potential can help us remain (go on being, endure, persist, continue in the same place, state, or condition, be left after removal, loss, or passage, stay behind after others have gone) in Jesus during it. Let's keep reading. Jesus, the Vine, has more to say about bearing fruit.

> "I am the vine, you are the branches; the one who remains in Me, and I in him bears much fruit, for apart from Me you can do nothing." (John 15:5)

We didn't save ourselves, and we can't prune ourselves and bear fruit by doubling down and trying really hard! To yield a fruitful harvest, we must remain in Jesus, the Word. But, oh, the blessed produce of our union. It's pleasing to our souls, it feeds other members of His body, and it beckons unbelievers to Christ.

Speaking of the faithless: Let's not confuse them with the fruitless. Jesus makes a distinction between them in this chapter. Earlier, we read that the Vinedresser inspects the branches and the fruitless are taken away. Those words "taken away" can also be translated as cleansed, which aligns with His teaching on cleansing in order to bear fruit. But Jesus is about to say something sobering about those who refuse to remain in Him that leaves no question as to the end the faithless will inherit.

> "If anyone does not remain in Me, he is thrown away like a branch and dries up; and they gather them and throw them into the fire, and they are burned." (John 15:6)

The hard truth is that many people who profess to be attached to Christ are actually attached to religious ideas and denominations. They're easily separated from Jesus when pressure comes their way because His life is not at work in them, and never has been. That said, differentiating between the fruitless and the faithful is hard work that's best left to the Master Gardener. It's far better for us to be busy abiding than it is for us to occupy ourselves trying to figure out which branches are pretending and which ones aren't.

Wonderful, startling, transformative things happen when we remain in Jesus and His words remain in us. Our wants begin to change, and our wills become transformed. We begin to ask Him for the very things He longs to do in and through us, and His life in us empowers us to love one another, which creates an ever-deepening friendship with God that allows us to share in His joy. Those aren't my promises—they're His.

[7] "If you remain in Me, and My words remain in you, ask whatever you wish, and it will be done for you. [8] My Father is glorified by this, that you bear much fruit, and so prove to be My disciples. [9] Just as the Father has loved Me, I also have loved you; remain in My love. [10] If you keep My commandments, you will remain in My love; just as I have kept My Father's commandments and remain in His love. [11] These things I have spoken to you so that My joy may be in you, and that your joy may be made full.

[12] "This is My commandment, that you love one another, just as I have loved you. [13] Greater love has no one than this, that a person will lay down his life for

his friends. [14] You are My friends if you do what I command you. [15] No longer do I call you slaves, for the slave does not know what his master is doing; but I have called you friends, because all things that I have heard from My Father I have made known to you. [16] You did not choose Me but I chose you, and appointed you that you would go and bear fruit, and that your fruit would remain, so that whatever you ask of the Father in My name He may give to you. [17] This I command you, that you love one another."

It's true: "What the world needs now is love, sweet love." The world is walking in darkness, not knowing the God who is Love because they continue to reject Jesus, the only way back to Him. They've swallowed the enemy's lie that peace can be found apart from God, and man can create a better world without Him. In their blind pursuit of this devilish mirage, they're increasingly quick to label anyone who says Jesus is the Way as being narrow-minded and a threat to society. We bristle at that response, don't we? Their offense offends us. And while it might make us want to back off into our safe little circles of like-minded believers, it's not Jesus's way. We're meant to keep coming toward them with Love the same way Love keeps coming for us. And we can. We can continue to love and witness to them, but only as far as we are abiding in Him.

[18] "If the world hates you, you know that it has hated Me before it hated you. [19] If you were of the world, the world would love you as its own; but because you are not of

the world, but I chose you out of the world, because of this the world hates you. [20] Remember the word that I said to you, 'A slave is not greater than his master.' If they persecuted Me, they will persecute you as well; if they followed My word, they will follow yours also. [21] But all these things they will do to you on account of My name, because they do not know the One who sent Me. [22] If I had not come and spoken to them, they would not have sin; but now they have no excuse for their sin. [23] The one who hates Me hates My Father also. [24] If I had not done among them the works which no one else did, they would not have sin; but now they have both seen and hated Me and My Father as well. [25] But this has happened so that the word that is written in their Law will be fulfilled: 'THEY HATED ME FOR NO REASON.'

[26] "When the Helper comes, whom I will send to you from the Father, namely, the Spirit of truth who comes from the Father, He will testify about Me, [27] and you are testifying as well, because you have been with Me from the beginning."

We shouldn't be surprised by the hate coming at us when Jesus told us to expect it—but to love authentically and effectively in its face, we must remember that we aren't left to our own resources, to love out of our own human nature. Holy Spirit is with us to empower us. Every generation needs both human and divine witness. When we remain in Jesus, the Spirit testifies to us, and we testify to the world. Let's keep going back. Let's discover the power of abiding in

Him. We have the Witness with us, and we are meant to be His witnesses in this world. We can't fail as long as we follow!

Dear Jesus,

We have read Your words about the necessity of abiding and remaining in You, and it's the desire of our hearts to do just that. You're our only hope of doing this. Help us. Grant us an ever-increasing hunger for Your Presence. Intellectually, we understand that You are the Word. Give us a fuller understanding of this glorious Truth, for it often boggles our minds. Reveal to us just how present You are through the Scriptures. Help us persist and endure both in the light and life they contain. We commit ourselves to remaining in You and giving attention to the Scriptures that Your Spirit might reveal more of You to us through the Word.

At the same time, Lord, despite our good intentions, we understand that Your faithful discipline will often be necessary as we seek to follow You. Thank You for loving us enough to correct us when we stray from Your will. Help us remain in You at all times, including these times of discipline, so that we can grow in You and in our understanding of Your ways.

Thank You for the powerful gift of Your Holy Spirit present in us, empowering us to abide in You. Our hope is in listening to Your Word and yielding to Your teachings. Alert us when we aren't responding to Your Voice, or worse still, resisting it. Forgive us and draw us closer still. We long for our friends and family, and the greater world around us, to know You. And we understand that

You will form Yourself in us and reach out to them through us, as we remain in You and Your teachings. We ask these things in Your sweet name, Jesus. Amen

For Discussion

1. Read the eighth chapter of Proverbs. Record as much as you see about the results (fruit) we can expect from meditating on Jesus.

2. Shellie wrote that we have the opportunity to yield to the Word and let it transform and prune us, or refuse to yield to the Word and face discipline. Did you agree with her conclusion and how she reached it? Why or why not?

3. Read Judges 9:13. Jesus is the new wine. (You can review that truth in chapter two of this study.) According to this verse, explain the two reactions the new wine produces and any commitment it leads you to make.

CHAPTER SIXTEEN

Press Your Supernatural Advantage

Dear John,

Remember when I told you about the endless power struggle going on here, with everyone vying for influence and jostling for position? We're constantly reminded that "it's not what you know, but who you know." That kind of thinking has a habit of permeating everything down here, and one can be pulled into it regardless of your distaste for the philosophy. Yes, John, that was experience speaking.

It so happens that the letters I've been writing to you are being included in a Bible study I'm putting together on your gospel. I'm investing my heart and soul in this work. I'm praying this book will find its way into the hands of many, many readers. I'm hoping it will encourage people to believe and keep believing in all Jesus is and all He has done so they can live with purpose, joy, and courage.

Mercy. Did that sound audacious to you? It did to me, once I set it down here in black and white, but we also say "go big or go home," and I like that attitude.

I've learned so much from your inspired writing that I long to share with others. And yet, despite all the time I've spent poring over your words, and regardless of the untold hours I've invested in this project, to even think about getting it out into the world requires me to wade right into that "who you know" business. Here's what I mean.

Our world is overflowing with books, and new releases hit the market daily. At the same time, studies suggest that while people are buying more books, they're actually reading fewer of them. I attribute that to the fact that we are a consumer-driven society, John, and advertisers are good at what they do. To be sure, the factors behind this reading decline are varied, but they don't speak to my point, so I won't get into them. I only bring the subject up to underscore the fact that competition for readers and shelf space is notably fierce, which does speak to our discussion.

When considering a manuscript proposal, publishers are interested in knowing if the author's network can help sell his or her books once they come to market. This leads to questions like, "Who do you know that will endorse your book?" Unfortunately, they're not asking for the names of family and friends. One big family reunion, and I'd be good to go!

The who-do-you-know game means publishers often ask authors to list "contacts they have that might help promote the book," as in media, print, online resources, etc. Again, Aunt Judy's newsletter and Cousin Michelle's blog don't qualify, unless they happen to command large audiences of readers. Papa and Mama don't count either, even if they are tireless supporters. (Papa loves giving away copies of my books, and Mama is always reminding him that doing so doesn't help my bottom line, but I'm okay with it. Their support is priceless.)

I had some fun there, John, but I think you see where I'm going. When publishers ask about an author's contacts, they're wanting to hear recognizable names of well-known influencers. The harsh reality is that who an author knows or doesn't know can play a big role in determining whether her work makes it into the hands of readers.

Ironically, John, I believe there truly is an advantage to realizing "it's not what you know, but who you know," and it truly is a game-changer—just not in the way it's typically understood. That old adage becomes solid-gold truth when applied to knowing God, believing in Jesus, and living in relationship with Holy Spirit. Now we're talking about a network that changes everything. Amen? I knew you'd agree. After all, I might say it differently, but it's all over your gospel.

That's it for now. Talk to you soon.

Hugs,
Shellie

Dear Reader,

For close to three years of His earthly ministry, Jesus had taught His disciples on a need-to-know basis. Together, they had traveled to and from Jerusalem more than once, with Jesus teaching both them and the crowds along the way. Then He and the disciples approached the holy city for the last time, and His private teachings shifted. The revelations to His most intimate friends deepened. Here in John 16, with the Cross and His resurrection within sight, the discourse of these final hours continues. Jesus remains hyper-focused on teaching them what they'll need to know in the days ahead. Soon, His friends will be on mission without His physical presence. It would behoove us to listen closely as He explains what they can expect, for that's exactly where we find ourselves.

> [1] "These things I have spoken to you so that you will not be led into sin. [2] They will ban you from the synagogue, yet an hour is coming for everyone who kills you to think that he is offering a service to God. [3] These things they will do because they have not known the Father nor Me. [4] But these things I have spoken to you, so that when their hour comes, you may remember that I told you of them. However, I did not say these things to you at the beginning, because I was with you.
>
> [5] "But now I am going to Him who sent Me; and none of you asks Me, 'Where are You going?' [6] But because I have said these things to you, grief has filled your heart. [7] But I tell you the truth: it is to your advantage that I am leaving; for if I do not leave, the Helper will not come to you; but if I go, I will send Him to you."

Jesus begins by reiterating what He had previously explained to the disciples: The Helper would be coming, in direct response to Jesus asking the Father to send Him. What a mysterious picture of the workings of the Trinity rests in that revelation! We have the Son asking the Father to send the Spirit. We see the Godhead in full agreement to make Heaven's greatest resource, God's Holy Spirit, available to those who believe. Jesus paid for and prayed for the great privilege we have of His Spirit indwelling and being available to us, and God answered His prayer. Now Jesus explains that going away will make things better for His friends than if He stayed with them physically, but the men struggle to comprehend this assurance and the Spirit's impact. Thankfully, the growth of the early Church under heavy persecution provides convincing evidence that the disciples did learn to embrace and rely on the Spirit. We can, too, friend! We're not destined to live with wobbly knees. Let's not allow what's happening around us to cause us to miss the privilege of seizing the promise of Holy Spirit being with us and for us. He is just as willing to strengthen us as we walk through these days as He was for generations past. Let's press our supernatural advantage in this life and learn to trust that Who we know immeasurably exceeds what we know.

Jesus had said many heartening things to the guys, but they were nursing their fears. And while we've confessed that we can relate, intentionally relying on Holy Spirit will fill us with the courage we need to persevere in our post-Christian world. Understanding His ministry and drawing on His resources will also encourage us to keep witnessing to this world when it seems far too dark to ever see the Light. Here's how Jesus describes the Spirit's work.

> [8] "And He, when He comes, will convict the world
> regarding sin, and righteousness, and judgment:
> [9] regarding sin, because they do not believe in Me; [10] and
> regarding righteousness, because I am going to the Father

and you no longer are going to see Me; [11] and regarding
judgment, because the ruler of this world has been judged."

Do note that the Spirit convicts the world regarding sin, righteousness, and judgment. Jesus doesn't say the Spirit would convict a few,
or some here and there, or those who are listening. We're told He
convicts the world. There is so much confidence in that promise for
us. We can take those words, engage our post-Christian society, and
stay the course. Believe, worship, witness, and repeat. Let our listeners
stake out their opposing positions. Truth tells us God is convicting
them of sin, righteousness, and judgment, even now. Will all be con-
verted? No, but all will be convicted. It's not your role or mine to push
conviction or conversion on anyone. It's God's. Our call is to press
our advantage in the Spirit, to love Him, and to love them. That's
more than enough to keep our hands full. So, how do we press our
advantage? Jesus is in the process of answering that question.

[12] "I have many more things to say to you, but you
cannot bear them at the present time. [13] But when He,
the Spirit of truth, comes, He will guide you into all the
truth; for He will not speak on His own, but whatever
He hears, He will speak; and He will disclose to you
what is to come. [14] He will glorify Me, for He will take
from Mine and will disclose it to you. [15] All things that
the Father has are Mine; this is why I said that He takes
from Mine and will disclose it to you."

A foundational truth of hearing and knowing Holy Spirit is
expecting Him to speak to those who are listening. Jesus said the

Spirit would guide us into all truth, that His Spirit would take what belongs to the Father and the Son and reveal it to us. This may sound harsh, but believers who say God doesn't speak to them are contradicting Jesus. I know, I know. You have questions. I do, too. So did the disciples.

> [16] "A little while, and you no longer are going to see Me; and again a little while, and you will see Me." [17] So some of His disciples said to one another, "What is this that He is telling us, 'A little while, and you are not going to see Me; and again a little while, and you will see Me'; and, 'because I am going to the Father'?" [18] So they were saying, "What is this that He says, 'A little while'? We do not know what He is talking about." [19] Jesus knew that they wanted to question Him, and He said to them, "Are you deliberating together about this, that I said, 'A little while, and you are not going to see Me, and again a little while, and you will see Me'? [20] Truly truly I say to you that you will weep and mourn, but the world will rejoice; you will grieve, but your grief will be turned into joy! [21] Whenever a woman is in labor she has pain, because her hour has come; but when she gives birth to the child, she no longer remembers the anguish because of the joy that a child has been born into the world. [22] Therefore you too have grief now; but I will see you again, and your heart will rejoice, and no one is going to take your joy away from you."

Earlier in this discourse Jesus promised to return to the disciples, explaining that He would come in the Spirit so they wouldn't have to go it alone. To that comforting revelation He now adds this one: His followers will have access to joy no one can take from them. How will all this happen? He's about to tell us.

> [23] "And on that day you will not question Me about anything. Truly, truly I say to you, if you ask the Father for anything in My name, He will give it to you. [24] Until now you have asked for nothing in My name; ask and you will receive, so that your joy may be made full. [25] "These things I have spoken to you in figures of speech; an hour is coming when I will no longer speak to you in figures of speech, but will tell you plainly about the Father. [26] On that day you will ask in My name, and I am not saying to you that I will request of the Father on your behalf; [27] for the Father Himself loves you, because you have loved Me and have believed that I came forth from the Father. [28] I came forth from the Father and have come into the world; again, I am leaving the world and going to the Father."

Jesus is describing a life of prayer. This is where the peace and joy He promises is found. We'll never know joy by simply knowing of Jesus. We find joy when we walk and talk with Jesus, when we ask and receive because we ask in His name. Did you hear Jesus's confidence in that last passage? He fully expects His people will be praying people who will ask of Him the things He already desires to give because they will be asking in His name. To ask in Jesus's name doesn't mean composing a wish list and tacking His name to the end of it like a magic charm. In antiquity, a name was a revelation of the person. It feels daunting to explain the significance here, but I'll try.

There was a time when the disciples didn't pray in Jesus's name, because they didn't know who He was. They didn't know His heart. Now, they do! Now, because they know what He is like, they know what the Father is like, for He and the Father are one, and they can ask accordingly.

We've been given the same revelation and opportunity: to know God the Father through Jesus the Son, the exact representation of His being (Hebrews 1:3). We have Jesus's life on record, and His Spirit lives in us. Jesus has prayed for and paid for our privilege of walking this world with His Spirit available to us through His Name. The more we talk to Him and walk with Him, the more like Him we become. He transforms us through relationship, and we begin to pray in His name. Prayers that align with Who He is, what He is doing, and what He wants to do.

> This is the confidence which we have before Him, that, if we ask anything according to His will, He hears us. And if we know that He hears us in whatever we ask, we know that we have the requests which we have asked from Him. (1 John 5:14–15)

Seeing the God of the Universe work in and through our lives as we pray produces joy the world can't offer. But wait, I think I hear the argument building in your mind. What if you've tried and failed to develop any kind of prayer life? What then? Ah, I've been there, and I can still go there, but Holy Spirit is teaching me things about prayer that I'm eager to share with you as we continue this study.

Right now, let's take heart in Jesus's closing words. His victory is ours, and through Him, we can learn how to live courageously when everything around us suggests we should be shaking in our boots.

> [29] His disciples said, "See, now You are speaking plainly and are not using any figure of speech. [30] Now we know that You know all things, and that You have no need for anyone to question You; this is why we believe that You came forth from God." [31] Jesus replied to them, "Do you now believe? [32] Behold, an hour is coming, and has already come, for you to be scattered, each to his own home, and to leave Me alone; and yet I am not alone, because the Father is with Me. [33] These things I have spoken to you so that in Me you may have peace. In the world you have tribulation but take courage; I have overcome the world."

I gleefully refuse to feel redundant for pointing out something here that was important enough for the Spirit of God to influence John to record it, time and again. Jesus knew He was speaking to people who had not arrived, so to speak. His future prayer warriors were currently fraidy cats, and still He loved them and looked forward to the day when His courage would be theirs because He had overcome the world. Take heart, believer. Jesus knows us thoroughly, and He loves us still!

Dear Jesus,

We rejoice in knowing we've not been left to go it alone in this world without You, and yet we so often do precisely that, whether intentionally, subconsciously, or because the enemy is distracting us from what's actually happening between our own ears. We confess that we're given to a misguided sense of responsibility to buck up and be courageous or scold ourselves into gratitude and joy through our own determined efforts. None of it works without You. Help us learn to press the great advantage we have through the gift of Your Spirit ever present with us. Stir us to open our mouths and call to You.

You have promised to guide us by Your Spirit. Forgive us for contradicting Your Word by claiming that You aren't speaking to us. The fault lies with us and our failure to listen and apply what You've already said. Give us ears to hear and a heart to respond in obedience that we might hear all the more. Remind us to expect You to speak to us as we position ourselves to hear.

We can see in Your Word that you expect us to pray in Your Name and that You intend to answer when we do. Forgive us for when we've hidden behind excuses for our weak or nonexistent prayer lives—and when we've begun to taste the joys of prayer, help us devote ourselves to further communion. Help us manage our time and form the discipline of coming to You with our words. Teach us the joys of being still, of listening and learning and experiencing the rhythms of prayer that are like a good conversation between friends. In Your sweet name, Jesus, in the revelation of all You are and all You've done, we pray. Amen.

For Discussion

1. Jesus says it is to our advantage that He is absent physically and the Holy Spirit is here. Do you feel like you're experiencing the reality of His words? Spend a

moment imagining what it would be like if Jesus was on the earth today. Do you think you'd be able to spend time with Him?

2. Read John 16:13–15. Do you think Holy Spirit teaches us things that aren't necessarily spelled out in the Word, but are truths we can deduce by judging whether the issue in question is in line with His revealed character? Or do you believe Holy Spirit teaches us concerning the Word already recorded and nothing more? What might be the danger of believing we are being given fresh revelation that isn't found in Scripture?

3. In John 16:17, the disciples are having a discussion among themselves. In verse 19, Jesus begins to speak to their concerns before they voice them. Read Malachi 3:16. What do these verses have in common, and what actions might they inspire in us?

CHAPTER SEVENTEEN

Pray with Otherworldly Confidence

Dear John,

For years now, I've been taking my coffee to the back porch or down to the dock behind my house in the early mornings to start my day with Jesus. He's always teaching me something new through the sights and sounds of nature that surround me as I pray. I enjoy watching the occasional bass jump and the egrets fishing for smaller fry among the cypress trees lining the lake bank. I'm not fond of the ridiculous numbers of buzzing and biting insects, but I do live in Louisiana. They come with the territory, and it's worth it. Oh, is it worth it!

Jesus has become my home, and this dedicated time with Him is now my favorite part of the day. And yet, a part of me is still amazed I can type out those words and mean every one of them! Honestly, John, I'd be afraid Holy Spirit would rap my fingers on these keys if I wasn't shooting straight here. I wonder if you ever felt that way when you were writing. (Right. I didn't think so.)

The truth is, John, I wanted to enjoy prayer long before I learned how, and now that it has become so precious, well, I guard that time like Hank with a bone. (Hank is my faithful companion and canine prayer partner. Although I suspect he isn't always praying when he closes his eyes.)

I love talking to people about prayer and telling them what I'm discovering. I long to help others discover the nourishment and stability prayer offers us far more quickly than I did. I believe they can, too!

More on prayer straight ahead, but for now, let's talk turtles. (I'll connect the two soon enough, John. Just go with me.)

I was driving not long ago when I spotted a box turtle right in the middle of the road. Not the best scenario. He needed to be hightailing it for the opposite side, and he was meandering at best. Bless him. I didn't like his odds. I pulled over, parked in a safe space, and checked for traffic before helping him across. I wish I could say I always stop on a dime to rescue turtles, John, but sometimes it's not safe to try. However, I had recently learned something interesting about box turtles—and that particular day, everything in me wanted to help that little guy make it home.

Did you know a box turtle will live its entire life within a one-mile radius of where it hatches? It's true. They're homebodies in every sense of the word. I read that if you remove a box turtle from its native territory and release it elsewhere, the poor box turtle will spend its entire life trying to get home. His whole life. Sobering, isn't it? Nature has so much truth to teach us if we'll listen.

Turtles looking for home remind me of fallen men and women walking this earth. Regardless of what mankind might profess, we'll never be content apart from getting back to God, for He is our Home. Unless we discover how to accept the life Jesus offers that leads us back into the friendship of God, we're bound to spend our entire lives searching for a Home that's wired into our very beings. Nothing compares to knowing Him. The glorious news is that we can experience Home here, through communing with Jesus in the Spirit, even as we travel to our Home there. Amen, John? Squeeze Jesus for me. I'll see y'all soon!

Hugs,
Shellie

Dear Reader,

Having announced to the disciples that He was leaving, and after explaining the blessings His death and resurrection would hold for them, Jesus turned and directed His next thoughts to the Father—in the disciples' hearing, while they were still processing. That reminds me of times when our kids were small and I'd talk to their daddy about them when I knew they were nearby and listening. The subject matter may have been about a positive character trait I saw developing in them, a good choice they had made, or even something of concern we needed to address. Other times, I might be recounting a harmful situation that could've turned out much worse, and I wanted them to hear my deep relief and gratitude. Regardless, those overheard conversations had common goals: to make Jessica and Phillip feel seen, secure, and confident in our love for them. I've done this more recently with our grandchildren.

Bless Jesus's great big heart. I believe He had similar intentions in our next passage when He lifted His voice to speak to His Father, and ours. The disciples were meant to overhear the Son discussing with the Father how much they were loved, valued, and chosen. We were meant to know it, too. Jesus will say as much in verse 20. Understanding Their shared love for us is where a confident prayer life begins.

> [1] Jesus spoke these things; and raising His eyes to heaven, He said, "Father, the hour has come; glorify Your Son, that the Son may glorify You, [2] just as You gave Him authority over all mankind, so that to all whom You have given Him, He may give eternal life."

Jesus opens His address to the Father by recognizing that His hour had come. I want to hold on to that point and savor it together as we close. Right now, please note that Jesus just said we are God's gift to Him. Jesus clearly wanted us to absorb this fact, for He'll repeat it several times before He concludes this prayer. We may feel more like a gag gift sometimes as we stumble and stutter, trying to pray without our minds slipping off to work on our to-do lists, but our poor estimation of ourselves doesn't diminish the truth. We're loved and chosen, and Jesus wants us to build our lives on that knowledge!

Hold that thought as we take in these next words. It's my life verse. If you're not familiar with the expression, a life verse simply means one that resonates with you in a different and deeper way. It feels more personal than others and has probably been instrumental in your faith. Years ago, Holy Spirit used John 17:3 to set me on a determined path to know God instead of settling for knowing *of* Him:

> "This is eternal life, that they may know You, the only true God, and Jesus Christ whom You have sent."

Eternal life isn't something that will happen to us later, in the life after this one. To quote Jesus Himself, eternal life is "knowing the only true God and Jesus Christ whom He has sent." The Cross made eternal life available to us now. This clearly stated divine relationship was purposed and purchased for us to enjoy. A shot of confidence to keep seeking such an intimate relationship with God lies straight ahead.

> [4] "I glorified You on the earth by accomplishing the work which You have given Me to do. [5] And now You, Father, glorify Me together with Yourself, with the glory which I had with You before the world existed. [6] I have revealed Your name to the men whom You gave Me out of the world; they were Yours and You gave them to Me, and they have followed Your word. [7] Now they have come to know that everything which You have given Me is from You; [8] for the words which You gave Me I have given to them; and they received them and truly understood that I came forth from You, and they believed that You sent Me. [9] I ask on their behalf; I do not ask on behalf of the world, but on the behalf of those whom You have given Me; because they are Yours; [10] and all things that are

Mine are Yours, and Yours are Mine; and I have been
glorified in them."

Wait a minute. Jesus said he *had been* glorified through His
disciples?! Are we talking about the same group of men? Is Jesus
really saying He was glorified through His stumbling, slow-to-
understand, one-step-forward-and-two-back, faith-challenged
friends? Yes, He most certainly did. We're looking at our encouragement. Grasp it with both hands. You and I are bringing glory
to Jesus by our faith. Not someday when we're fully mature and
perfect. Now. We're bringing Jesus glory *now*, and He is with us,
watching over us, as it happens!

> [11] "I am no longer going to be in the world; and yet they
> themselves are in the world, and I am coming to You.
> Holy Father, keep them in Your name, the name which
> You have given Me, so that they may be one just as We
> are. [12] While I was with them, I was keeping them in
> Your name which You have given Me; and I guarded
> them and not one of them perished except the son of
> destruction, so that the Scripture would be fulfilled."

Jesus fulfilled Scripture by keeping or "guarding" the disciples?
That's interesting and monumentally important to our growing
faith. Jesus couldn't have been saying that He had guarded the
physical lives of His disciples and lost no one but Judas. We can be
sure of this because He says one of them has already perished, and
at this point Judas had yet to betray Jesus and kill himself!

It was Judas's soul that had perished, as Scripture said it would, and all the while, Jesus had kept and protected the disciples' faith. Likewise, when Jesus asks Father to keep us, He is asking Father to protect our faith, not our physical lives. I hope you didn't read that as a disappointment. It's actually extremely good news. For "What does it profit a man to gain the whole world and forfeit his soul?" (Mark 8:36 ESV). So, how is His prayer answered? How is our faith protected? Let's keep reading to find out.

> [13] "But now I am coming to You; and these things I speak in the world, that they may have My joy fulfilled in themselves. [14] I have given them Your word; and the world has hated them, because they are not of the world, just as I am not of the world. [15] I do not ask You to take them out of the world, but that you keep them from the evil one. [16] They are not of the world, just as I am not of the world. [17] Sanctify them in the truth; Your word is truth. [18] As You sent Me into the world, so I have sent them into the world. [19] And for their sake I consecrate Myself, that they also may be sanctified in truth. [20] I do not ask for these only, but also for those who will believe in Me through their word; [21] that they may all be one; just as You, Father, are in Me and I in You, that they also may be in Us, so that the world may believe that You sent Me."

We are sanctified (kept from stumbling and our faith made complete) by the Word of God (John 17:17). Truth Himself secured our relationship to God and made provision for the growth He desires in us. It's all Jesus. That's worthy of a shout right there. This is the foundation for discovering the blessing of intimate relationship through prayer. We find enduring strength and ongoing joy by placing our confidence in this otherworldly prayer partner who is keeping us and sanctifying us through our communion with Him, and not in our prayers that seem to fall woefully short in our own ears.

Remember when Jesus opened this prayer by saying "the hour had come"? I used to hear that as Jesus steeling Himself in the shadow of the Cross. I don't anymore. I believe Jesus was rejoicing! I believe He was thrilling to the reality ahead. Father and Son had planned for this hour, they had joyfully anticipated this hour, and it had come. Mankind's access to God would be restored, and all the blessings that came with this divinely secured relationship awaited believers through the power of the indwelling Spirit.

Finally, the One with the answers would indwell those who didn't have them, present and available for them to turn to with their requests.

Finally, the One with the strength to prevail would live to fortify the weak, and His inadequate believers could call on the One who is more than enough!

Finally, Living Water would flow from within every believer, bubbling up and splashing over those around them.

I could keep listing benefits, for they are endless, but the pinnacle of joy lies in understanding that none of it rests on our ability to ask just right, knock acceptably, and seek perfectly. The ever-present availability of the Cross's blessings rests on the same perfect shoulders that bore it to Calvary's hill. Disregarding our ineptitude and reveling in His finished work is the key to building a prayer life that brims with otherworldly confidence, and it's a life that Jesus fully intends us to discover.

²⁵ "O righteous Father, even though the world does not know You, I know You, and these know that You have sent Me. ²⁶ I made known to them Your name, and I will continue to make it known, that the love with which You have loved Me may be in them, and I in them." (ESV)

We can find rest here, in Jesus's joyful announcement that He has made God known to us and He is fully committed to continuing to reveal the Father to us through His Spirit. Let's pray.

Dear Jesus,

Your own words demonstrate how much You looked forward to us experiencing the joy of intimate fellowship with You and the Father. You knew the blessings of divine companionship that awaited believers on the other side of the Cross, and You paid the most unimaginable cost to purchase this gift of access for us. Teach us how to use it! Form the prayer life You enjoyed with Father in us. We confess that we often live so far below this privilege of our new birth. Convict us where we are resigned to weak, ineffective, hit-or-miss prayer lives. Teach us to pray out of the knowledge of what You have done instead of praying in a way that tries to earn what You've already freely given.

Thank You for the opportunity to know You and Your Father through Your Spirit. Circumcise our hearts to want more and more of this divine communion. And thank You for adding those incredibly sweet words about "praying for those also who would believe through the disciples' testimony." We're encouraged to know that You prayed specifically for us.

We belong to You, Jesus. We are not the same as the humans around us who haven't passed from death into life. Help us live out of Your eternal life that lives in us! Help us listen to You. Help us take refuge in You and be refreshed by You, that we might live in such unity with You and with each other that the world would know that You live! Jesus, it's in Your mighty and holy name that we ask these things. Because we rejoice to know they align with Your will, we thank You now for answering them. Amen.

For Discussion

1. In John 17:1, Jesus prayed for God to glorify Him so that He could give glory back to the Father. Although God would soon resurrect Jesus and glorify Him in Heaven, the Father also answered that prayer and glorified Jesus on Earth. Read Matthew 27:19, 51–52. Record the ways you see God glorifying Jesus during His Passion.

2. Jesus also said more than once in this prayer that He was sent by God. Find and record five of these instances. Why might Jesus have felt so strongly about emphasizing that He was on mission from God that He repeatedly mentioned this origin of His ministry before the disciples?

3. Read John 17:13 and Hebrews 12:2. What do you think is Jesus's joy that He wants to give to us?

CHAPTER EIGHTEEN

Commit to a Biblically Sound Defense

D ear John,

Some people down here say all dogs go to Heaven. Other folks don't seem to care. I belong to the first group. If there aren't dogs in Heaven, spare me. By the time I find out, I suspect it won't matter near as much.

Not that I've always been a dog person. We had dogs when I was growing up, but they were "yard dogs" living on the edges of my world. Everything changed when my son placed a little brown ball of fur wearing a bright red collar in my arms. That chocolate lab puppy was a Christmas gift. Our two kids had left for college, and being the last to leave, Phillip thought our empty nest needed some canine companionship.

I named the wee thing Dixie Belle. She and I were instant buds, and over time, she became my early-morning prayer partner and my loyal, self-appointed, devoted-to-the-point-of-neurosis body-guard. Dixie was insanely defensive of me (emphasis on insane). She would've fought a bear for me. Or the shadow of a bear. Or the rug if a corner of it was rolled up wrong on the back porch. In Dixie's mind, anything could be a threat to her human mama, and she was dedicated to vanquishing all comers—unless they discovered her sweet spot. Dixie's over-the-top protectiveness was bested only by her tennis ball fetish. Had a potential villain thrown a tennis ball in the opposite direction, it would've been "Adios, Dixie" and open season on yours truly.

Craziness aside, I loved that old girl. I cried a river when she went to Heaven, declaring I didn't want another dog. So we got two.

Beaux and Mo were the Lab puppies I soon nicknamed Double Trouble. Our house, our porch, and our yard were at their mercy—but they had none. The busy brothers joyfully chewed up everything in sight before they contracted a highly contagious and potentially deadly virus called Parvo. Beaux recovered. Mo didn't. To comfort Beaux (and his human parents), we took in Hank, a brother from the same litter. While this effectively soothed all of our hearts, Hank's arrival had the unexpected consequence of ratcheting the destructive puppy behavior up to unprecedented levels. I'd often heard that if you can live through a Lab's first two years, you'll have yourself a really good dog. We had serious doubts about whether we could hang in for the duration. Had we not installed an electric fence to prevent the canine terrorists from wreaking havoc on the neighborhood, I'd be writing you from jail. (Not joking.)

I loved those pups in spite of themselves. Things eventually settled down, and for several years the three of us were a happy writing tribe, as well-adjusted as two dogs and a writer human could be. In the evenings Phil would come in from farming, and I would catch him up on our daily adventures. Then Beaux, our gorgeous golden hunk of canine, disappeared without a trace. I like to think whoever took him, if that's what happened, has loved him as much as we did. I can't let myself consider the other scenarios that have crossed my mind.

So, here we are again. The home office consists of one writer and one emotionally challenged guard dog. Phil and I don't know if Hank saw something traumatic when Beaux disappeared or if he just misses his brother, but he has since developed his own issues. He buries his chew toys and whines because they're missing. When he isn't pacing and moaning on my writing porch as I try to work, he's chasing fishing boats away from the dock and anxiously objecting to the neighbors walking outside their own homes. (The nerve of them.) But here's the kicker: Dog on Duty will even bristle up at my husband or me if we surprise him in the yard and we're any distance away. Granted, once we call to him and the big sweetheart realizes his mistake, he drops his tail between his legs and pulls his ears way back as if to say, "Sorry, folks. My bad."

The truth is, John, I wish I could be as quick to realize when I'm squaring off at the wrong target. I know we don't war "against flesh and blood" but against the "world forces of darkness" (Ephesians 6:12). The problem is, politics, entertainment, and breaking news can blind my better reasoning and make me crazy combative in a split second. If I'm not on my guard against the real enemy, I'll see people who sorely need Jesus as the threat, and we both know barking like a mad dog doesn't make one an effective witness for Christ. (Sorry, Hank. You know I love you!)

All that to say, I appreciate your careful account of Jesus's last hours. Your record has helped me see how to share the Gospel and defend it without being vengeful to those who oppose it. I've got a way to go, John, but I do believe I'm headed in the right direction. Much obliged!

Hugs,
Shellie

Dear Reader,

We're about to read the account of Jesus's arrest in the garden. He'll be betrayed by a friend who uses his intimate knowledge of Jesus's personal habits to betray Him to an angry crowd of Roman soldiers, temple police, chief priests, and Pharisees.

¹ When Jesus had spoken these words, He went away with His disciples across the ravine of the Kidron, where there was a garden which He entered with His disciples. ² Now Judas, who was betraying Him, also knew the place, because Jesus had often met there with His disciples. ³ So Judas, having obtained the Roman cohort and officers from the chief priests and the Pharisees, came there with lanterns, torches, and weapons. ⁴ Jesus therefore, knowing all the things that were coming upon Him, came out into the open and said to them, "Whom are you seeking?" ⁵ They answered Him, "Jesus the Nazarene." He said to them, "I am He." And Judas also, who was betraying Him, was standing with them. ⁶ Now

then, when He said to them, "I am He," they drew back
and fell to the ground. (John 18)

Jesus's enemies fell to the ground at His word. Hold that thought. We'll return to it as we conclude our study on this chapter.

> [7] He then asked them again, "Whom are you seeking?"
> And they said, "Jesus the Nazarene." [8] Jesus answered,
> "I told you that I am He; so if you are seeking Me, let
> these men go on their way." [9] This took place so that the
> word which He spoke would be fulfilled: "Of those
> whom You have given Me I lost not one."

Conservative estimates tell us this multitude was comprised of three hundred to six hundred torch-toting, weapon-wielding men seeking one man. It must've been an intimidating sight, just like the devil intended. Intimidation is a favorite tool of the enemy, but Jesus's example is pure gold for those of us living in an angry and anxious culture that's bent on erasing the Unerasable God. See Jesus, calm and measured, advocating to be taken alone and for His disciples to be released. Their Keeper is ours, and He lives in us to grant us His supernatural perspective and resolve. Jesus keeps us still.

> [10] Then Simon Peter, since he had a sword, drew it and
> struck the high priest's slave, and cut off his right ear;
> and the slave's name was Malchus. [11] So Jesus said to

Peter, "Put the sword into the sheath; the cup which the
Father has given Me, am I not to drink it?" [12] So the
Roman cohort, the commander, and the officers of the
Jews arrested Jesus and bound Him, [13] and brought Him
to Annas first; for he was the father-in-law of Caiaphas,
who was high priest that year.

The record of Peter denying Jesus is straight ahead in this chapter, but we won't be spending our time on that story. Instead, I'd
like for us to consider that choosing the safety of anonymity over
his testimony was not Peter's first move. Let's look into what implications that may hold for us.

Before Peter's infamous denial came this initial instinct to fight. I
wonder if Peter was confused when Jesus corrected him over his rash
but well-intentioned defense. Perhaps the feisty fisherman expected
an "attaboy" instead of a "down, boy." Could this moment have been
a contributing factor to Peter denying Jesus a short time later? The
Word doesn't say, but I think it's possible. And now I'm speaking from
personal experience. It's easy to find myself in Peter's story.

When I see the world attacking everything I hold sacred and
working to oust all mention of God from our society, it's all I can
do not to jump into the fray without first pausing and looking to
Jesus for direction. I'm Peter, finding it easier to fight for Jesus than
to die with Him! I might not slice off the world's ears, but left to
my own impulses, I can fill them with words that damage the cause
of the Gospel as surely as Peter's sword wounded that slave.

On the other hand, when I'm confused as to how to combat
this world's growing darkness without slicing off those figurative

ears, I can be tempted to withdraw from it, and that response can effectively hide my light, even if that's not my intention. If this rings true for you, here's some encouraging news for both of us: In the years following Christ's resurrection, Peter learned how to give a defense of the Gospel without taking vengeance on those who opposed it. Consider his words from 1 Peter 3:15–16:

> But sanctify Christ as Lord in your hearts, always being ready to make a defense to everyone who asks you to give an account for the hope that is in you, but with gentleness and respect; and keep a good conscience so that in the thing in which you are slandered, those who disaparage your good behavior in Christ will be put to shame.

So, Impulsive Peter learned how to defend the Gospel with gentleness, reverence, and a clean conscience? How foreign that approach sounds compared to so much of our public debate! And yet, God's Word has no pass to offer us twenty-first-century Christ followers. Ladies, Jesus won't hold our earrings while we get up in the flesh and act crazy. He won't overlook or condone sin, but He will empower us to respond to the moment in His strength and wisdom, with His restraint, when we yield to His Spirit. Do we live in an increasingly godless world that seems to be intentionally destabilizing our society and normalizing depravity while painting Christians as the gravest threat to democracy and peace? We absolutely do, but we're still called to grow in our ability to defend the Gospel, just as Peter did, even now. And we can start by grasping the foundational truth Jesus lays out next.

³³ Therefore Pilate entered the Praetorium again, and summoned Jesus and said to Him, "You are the King of the Jews?" ³⁴ Jesus answered, "Are you saying this on your own, or did others tell you about Me?" ³⁵ Pilate answered, "I am not a Jew, am I? Your own nation and the chief priests handed You over to me; what have You done?" ³⁶ Jesus answered, "My kingdom is not of this world. If My kingdom were of this world, My servants would be fighting so that I would not be handed over to the Jews; but as it is, My kingdom is not of this realm." (John 18)

Over and again, we find Jesus telling the disciples that His Kingdom is not of this world, and He didn't come to overthrow the power structures of their day. With longsuffering love and patience, He repeatedly defined His mission: He came to reign in the hearts of men and women who would live as representative citizens of a Kingdom that can't be seen or defeated, a Kingdom characterized by love and unity that would spread with every heart that yielded to Him. Because this wasn't what they wanted to hear, or what they'd been taught to expect, the disciples struggled with this invisible-kingdom teaching for the duration of Jesus's earthly ministry. (Where did we put that mirror, right?)

Centuries have come and gone, and we're still wrestling with that truth, still needing constant reminders that Jesus's Kingdom is not of this world. When will we learn that the Kingdom we belong to is a spiritual one? God can certainly give us physical power and health. He can absolutely choose to give us material riches and favor to suit His purposes when these things align with His will, but it has been said that the things of this world are not the best things, and God repays with the best—Himself! He is our reward.

Prestige and favor do not describe the Kingdom Jesus established on Earth before the eyes of the disciples, despite their incessant clamoring for Him to put the world in its place! God's Kingdom demands the hearts of men and women, not their governments or their institutions. These will be given over to Him only as hearts are given over to Jesus.

There are tragic consequences to not understanding the nature of the Kingdom we've inherited. For starters, we rob our own souls when we try to make the promises of God's spiritual Kingdom apply to our physical lives, but the ripple effect of our inevitable disappointment also leaves us with narrow, undernourished souls that render us incapable of pointing a hurting world to Christ, the Healer.

The day is coming when the kingdoms of this world will become the kingdoms of our God (Revelation 11:15), but that happens on the final day, Judgment Day. Not grasping this truth leaves us fighting the wrong battles and making enemies of those we're called to reach. It can preoccupy us with wanting Jesus to vindicate us before the world, anxious for Him to prove that we're right on the issues of our day, and those who oppose us are wrong. Is it not true that once we start down that path we can even let our desire to prevail in arguments with unbelievers overrun our desire to win them to Jesus? Forgive us, Lord. Fighting the wrong battle or bowing out of the public debate are both disastrous choices, and neither build the Kingdom. We're called to engage with the supernatural weapons of our spiritual inheritance.

If we'll fortify ourselves with the worship of God and the Word of God, the Holy Spirit will teach us how to be angry at sin without sinning. We can learn to buttress our lives in prayer as we fight against the powers of darkness and seek the prosperity of the true Kingdom. Instead of being surprised that a fallen world acts like what it is, we can ask Holy Spirit to teach us how to speak truth in love without compromising the Gospel.

Without a doubt, it'd take another book to thoroughly address how to live in this world without being part of it, but that's not the book I feel called to write. My point in a nutshell? Knowing when to speak and when to keep silent, how much to say and to whom—these are impossible assignments without present-tense, Holy-Spirit-led discernment.

Blowing our lids (and our witness) will always be the easier choice when we're attacked, but the challenge of yielding and being led also holds unparalleled blessing. Why? Because the company of Jesus is the reward of continually resorting to the Spirit. His presence brings peace and joy to our lives while the world boils around us.

We're bound to be poor, inept, sword-wielding saviors without listening to Jesus. But when we're yielded to Him, we are Light bearers steadily revealing truth—not because we know what to say and do, but because He does.

> ³⁷ Therefore Pilate said to Him, "So You are a king?" Jesus answered, "You say correctly that I am a king. For this purpose I have been born, and for this I have come into the world: to testify to the truth. Everyone who is of the truth listens to My voice." ³⁸ Pilate said to Him,

"What is truth?" And after saying this, he came out again to the Jews and said to them, "I find no grounds at all for charges in His case."

Just like Jesus and the disciples who came before us, we live in the tension of a Kingdom that is coming although it has already arrived. Jesus spoke truth here and truth prevailed. Pilate could find no fault in Him. We saw the same thing earlier in our chapter when Jesus spoke a word to those who came to arrest Him, and they promptly fell to the ground. Jesus proved that they were powerless against Him even as He let them lead Him away. Let's keep God's Word in our hearts and have the law of kindness on our lips as we speak to the issues of our day, committing ourselves to the proper defense of the right kingdom, that truth might prevail again in the hearts of those Christ died to redeem!

She opens her mouth with wisdom,
and the teaching of kindness is on her tongue.
(Proverbs 31:26 ESV)

Dear Jesus,

We are comforted by remembering that You are our Keeper. As surely as You watched over Your earliest disciples, You are watching over us today. We've trusted You with our souls. We know that You are ours and we are Yours, and we'll be with You throughout eternity. And yet, we now confess what You already know. We struggle to trust You with our physical lives. We default so easily to fear of the future and what life will look like for our kids and grandkids. Forgive us. We know You've chosen us and our loved ones for these days, and You are willing to equip us to live them. Help us to model an otherworldly peace that brings You much glory.

Your closest friends on Earth had trouble understanding the Kingdom You came to establish. We do, too. Oh, how desperately we need You. We ask for wisdom, believing that it's Your desire to grant it. Thank You! Alert us whenever we are squaring off against the wrong enemy. Remind us we fight the darkness from a victory You've already secured, and remind us to come to You daily that You might equip us to overcome evil.

Towards that goal, Lord, we commit ourselves to finding nourishment and strength in Your Word. Help us. Circumcise our hearts to love Your Word more tomorrow than we do today. Teach us to hide Your Word in our hearts that we wouldn't sin against You, and help us learn to speak Truth that prevails in our day. When we do see You face-to-face, grant that we might come with a harvest of souls because we learned to fight the good fight the right way! In Your almighty name we pray, Jesus. Amen.

For Discussion

1. Read John 18:1–11. Continuing in the vein of the discussion we had at the end of chapter seventeen, record anything you find in this passage that reveals Jesus being glorified before the religious leaders and the Roman authorities during His arrest.

2. In the garden of Gethsemane, Jesus prayed for His Father to "take this cup from me." How does

knowing Jesus wanted to avoid the Cross make you feel? Now, review what He told Peter at His arrest in John 18:11 and read Psalm 116:13. What do you think had transpired between Father and Son that caused Jesus to be willing to embrace His cup, and what can it teach us?

3. Jesus conversed with Pilate, the Roman governor (John 18:33–38), differently than He did with the High Priest, who should have known Him (John 18:19–24). Read both passages and record any takeaway you may have after comparing the two.

CHAPTER NINETEEN

Despise the Shame

D ear John,
There's a story from my childhood that Mama loves to tell. You may enjoy it, too. It seems my family was headed to church, yet again, and little Shellie felt like we were overdoing it. The details are lost to time, but I wouldn't be surprised if this incident came at the end of one of our customary two-week revivals. Here's some necessary backstory: I had quite the speech impediment as a child, which is ironic for someone who grew up to be a speaker and Bible teacher. Jesus does like to use our weakness to showcase His strength. Amen?

As Mama tells it, Little Shellie's response to yet another trip to the Lord's house was a deep sigh and an equally dramatic announcement, "Chuch, chuch, chuch, that's all we ever do!" My parents may have chuckled at my delivery, but they couldn't quibble with my observation. If we weren't gathering with the faithful at Melbourne, we were at Riverside, sitting under my Papaw Stone's preaching. Funny thing is, John, when I look back on those early years, all my memories are colored in shades of gold.

I loved our sheltered life and the shared faith of our community. I wouldn't have known to call it security, but I now know that's what I felt. Besides, I had no idea everyone's lives didn't revolve around the church. Of course, with time, that little girl became a teenager and discovered that a whole other world did indeed exist. I still enjoyed my people, at least when I was with them. But I was now exposed to a different kind of living. Some of my new friends' parents seemed cooler than mine, and they didn't take Jesus so terribly seriously. It made me wonder why we did.

As far as I could see, there was nothing cool about my family. I was perpetually embarrassed by the things I wasn't permitted to do and the places I wasn't allowed to go. I know; such restrictions are a far cry from the persecution you early believers endured when it was your lives on the line and not just your teenage reputations. I can't imagine what that was like for you and your friends, and I don't know what it's like for the many believers around the globe who are still being tortured and killed for following Jesus. (Then again, some say we'll see that level of persecution in my own country before He returns. So I may just find out. Only God knows.)

I suppose those cringey teenage years are when I began trying to live with "Jesus on the side." I coined that phrase to describe the folly of trying to have just enough Jesus to get to Heaven without having Him take over one's whole life. (Yes, it now sounds ridiculous to me, too.) It didn't then, but you know what that compartmentalized faith gave me, don't you, John? I'll say it anyway: Nothing. It gave me nothing. No peace. No joy. No comfort. Trying to live for Jesus without living with Jesus is a sad exercise in futility. The life I now know, the one worth living, has come in learning to openly "despise the shame," as Scripture says, and invite Jesus to help Himself to all of me. To choose Jesus over every lesser thing, to ask Him to be in all my thoughts, to privately and publicly own my hunger for Him—this has been my path to discovering the ever-flowing Well that quenches my thirsty soul.

I realize I'm not telling you anything you don't know, John, but it sure is fun walking down memory lane together. Thanks for putting up with me! I'll be back.

Hugs,
Shellie

Dear Reader,

Stating the obvious here, but our secular world would like nothing more than to shame Jesus lovers into silence and anonymity. They spotlight the misguided and unbalanced actions of some people who call themselves Christians in an attempt to paint all Christ followers with the same brush. They protest that declaring Jesus to be the only way to God is divisive and intolerant, and they're increasingly adamant that such "narrow" beliefs are a threat to peace and democracy. Friend, to discover the soul peace and settled joy of Christ's Presence, we must learn to despise that shame.

By despising the shame, I mean we must disregard it and consider it inconsequential, having no bearing on our faith, and incapable of influencing or altering the way we live as we continue to share the Gospel. Jesus is the Way, the Truth, and the Life. He is the exact representation of the invisible God. He is the great I Am and there is no other. Before we begin unpacking this chapter, let's spell out this goal using Jesus's victory as our model, as recorded in Hebrews 12:1–2.

> Therefore, since we are surrounded by so great a cloud of witnesses, let us also lay aside every weight, and sin which clings so closely, and let us run with endurance the race that is set before us, looking to Jesus, the founder and perfecter of our faith, who for the joy that was set before him endured the cross, despising the shame, and is seated at the right hand of the throne of God. (ESV)

What a glorious description of our risen Savior despising the shame we're about to read about here in John! This chapter holds some of the hardest passages to read in all of God's Word, and yet the Creator willingly endured it at the hands of His created. Let's see what we can learn from His example.

> [1] So Pilate then took Jesus and had Him flogged. [2] And the soldiers twisted together a crown of thorns and placed it on His head, and put a purple cloak on Him; [3] and they repeatedly came up to Him and said, "Hail, King of the Jews!" and slapped Him in the face again and again. [4] And then Pilate came out again and said to them, "See, I am bringing Him out to you so that you will know that I find no grounds at all for charges in His case." [5] Jesus then came out, wearing the crown of thorns

and the purple robe. And Pilate said to them, "Behold, the Man!" (John 19)

"Behold the Man," indeed. I don't know if Pilate was trying to appeal to the crowd's pity by presenting a flogged and bleeding Jesus, but it's worth noting that His haters had none for Him and they'll have none for us. We'd do well not to look to unredeemed men for mercy they can't give. Proverbs 12:10 reads *even the compassion of the wicked is cruel,* but Psalm 103:13–14 reassures us of God's compassion.

> Just as a father has compassion on his children, so the LORD has compassion on those who fear Him. For He Himself knows our form; He is mindful that we are nothing but dust.

God's compassion for us is all the more reason to resort to Him when we're attacked for our beliefs. In Him, we'll find the solace and strength we need to walk with Jesus against the opposition of our day and keep witnessing to the Truth.

> [6] So when the chief priests and the officers saw Him, they shouted, saying, "Crucify, crucify!" Pilate said to them, "Take Him yourselves and crucify Him; for I find no grounds for charges in His case!" [7] The Jews answered him, "We have a law, and by that law He ought to die, because He made Himself out to be the Son of God!" [8] Therefore when Pilate heard this statement, he was even more afraid; [9] and he entered the Praetorium again and

said to Jesus, "Where are You from?" But Jesus gave him no answer. [10] So Pilate said to Him, "Are you not speaking to me? Do You not know that I have authority to release You, and I have authority to crucify You?" [11] Jesus answered him, "You would have no authority over Me at all, if it had not been given to you from above; for this reason the one who handed Me over to you has the greater sin."

Whoa. Pilate grew increasingly anxious, didn't he? I don't believe he is asking Jesus what city he hails from, as Christ's hometown is common knowledge at this point in the timeline. Remember, Pilate's wife had already warned him about this Jesus. I believe the question was deeper, that it was more like, *"Are you from this world or beyond it?"* With His answer, Jesus gives us another lesson in how we, too, can learn to despise the shame: by reminding ourselves that no authority on Earth can exert power over those who belong to God that He hasn't allowed for His purposes.

Our next passage is lengthy, and our minds tend to wander. I get it, but stay with me. Let's do Jesus the honor of taking in all the sorrow and pain He endured on our behalf. The practice itself holds a lesson for us. I'll explain below.

[16] So he then handed Him over to them to be crucified. [17] They took Jesus, therefore, and He went out, carrying His own cross, to the place called the Place of a Skull, which in Hebrew is called, Golgotha. [18] There they crucified Him, and with Him two other men, one on either side, and Jesus in between. [19] Now Pilate also wrote an

inscription and put it on the cross. It was written: "JESUS THE NAZARENE, THE KING OF THE JEWS." [20] Therefore many of the Jews read this inscription, because the place where Jesus was crucified was near the city; and it was written in Hebrew, Latin, and in Greek. [21] So the chief priests of the Jews were saying to Pilate, "Do not write, 'The King of the Jews'; rather, write that He said, 'I am King of the Jews.'" [22] Pilate answered, "What I have written, I have written."

[23] Then the soldiers, when they had crucified Jesus, took His outer garments and made four parts: a part to each soldier, and the tunic also; but the tunic was seamless, woven in one piece. [24] So they said to one another, "Let's not tear it, but cast lots for it, to decide whose it shall be." This happened so that the Scripture would be fulfilled: "THEY DIVIDED MY GARMENTS AMONG THEMSELVES, AND THEY CAST LOTS FOR MY CLOTHING." Therefore the soldiers did these things. [25] Now beside the cross of Jesus stood His mother, His mother's sister, Mary the wife of Clopas, and Mary Magdalene. [26] So when Jesus saw His mother, and the disciple whom He loved standing nearby, He said to His mother, "Woman, behold, your son!" [27] Then He said to the disciple, "Behold, your mother!" And from that hour the disciple took her into his own household.

[28] After this, Jesus, knowing that all things had already been accomplished, in order that the Scripture would be fulfilled, said, "I am thirsty." [29] A jar full of sour wine was standing there; so they put a sponge full

of the sour wine on a branch of hyssop and brought it
up to His mouth. [30] Therefore when Jesus had received
the sour wine, He said, "It is finished!" And He bowed
His head and gave up His spirit.

I once heard it said that as hard as it is to behold what sin did
to Jesus physically, it's only a picture of what our sin costs the
Godhead spiritually. Jesus despised the shame of all that torture,
mockery, and barbary, and He insisted on tasting the whole of it.
In both Mark and Matthew's accounts of the crucifixion, we're told
that Jesus was offered vinegar mingled with myrrh early in those
horrible hours on the Cross, but He wouldn't drink it because the
concoction was used to dull the senses and make the pain more
bearable. Jesus would take no shortcuts and accept no escape from
the full brunt of the suffering He was called to taste on our behalf,
however small the solace. Only at the bitter end did Jesus admit his
thirst and accept a drink of sour wine (without the addition of the
painkilling myrrh) and that was to fulfill the Scriptures (verse 28).
After drinking the sour wine Jesus announced, "It is finished."

Anyone with a tendency to keep trying to earn the grace that's
been freely given to us in Christ (I'm raising my hand, here!) would
do well to repeat His words to ourselves day in and day out. What
can we do to secure this great salvation and approach the living
God? Nothing. It is done. *Selah*. We can only live out of it gratefully
and pass it on.

Our temptation is to inoculate ourselves against the depravity
around us by closing ranks and hiding in plain sight with like-
minded souls instead of engaging lost souls destined for judgment.

But Christ's example teaches us to despise the shame of this world by offering our lives as altars to fully taste the pain and sorrow of those trapped in the darkness. By resorting to the Spirit, we can remain in the game, stay in the conversation, be present in the public square, and fight from victory.

And now, one short passage and a closing thought...

> [38] Now after these things Joseph of Arimathea, being a disciple of Jesus, but a secret one for fear of the Jews, requested of Pilate that he might take away the body of Jesus; and Pilate granted permission. So he came and took away His body. [39] Nicodemus, who had first come to Him by night, also came, bringing a mixture of myrrh and aloes, about a hundred litras weight. [40] So they took the body of Jesus and bound it in linen wrappings with the spices, as is the burial custom of the Jews. [41] Now in the place where He was crucified there was a garden, and in the garden was a new tomb in which no one had yet been laid. [42] Therefore because of the Jewish day of preparation, since the tomb was nearby, they laid Jesus there.

Joseph may have harbored a fear of the leaders as a new believer, but he would've known that after asking for Jesus's body he'd have no place left to hide. Nicodemus first came to Jesus by night, but he was now willing to clean and anoint the abused body of His Lord, wrap it in linen, and accompany Joseph to the tomb, bearing the precious burden for anyone to see. Both of these men learned to despise the shame. With God's help, we can, too.

Dear Jesus,

We confess that we like to be liked and we aren't immune to the ridicule and rejection of men. Help us. Teach us how to despise the shame of this world and count everything as loss for the glory of knowing You. We won't do it without tasting and discovering that everything pales in Your Presence, so help us draw aside with You regularly and walk with You consistently. Help us order our schedules in a way that allows us to drink deeply of Your mercies so that we'll have fresh eternal Truth to offer the flesh-and-blood people around us instead of looking to them for approval or affection.

We need wisdom and courage to keep standing in Your truth when it conflicts with current opinion and the culture is bent on drowning out our voices. Help! We're powerless to bear up under our own strength, but we are overcomers through Yours. Remind us to look to You as the battle is raging instead of fighting from our own resources. And when persecution comes, remind us that You're our keeper. Regardless of the form it takes, no opposition comes against us that You haven't permitted.

Help us not shrink back from suffering, but to feel the world's death throes and fully engage with hurting people who are destroying themselves and others in blind allegiance to the enemy's lies. Teach us not to retreat but to advance in love, despising the shame, that we might partner with You to rescue those held captive by deceit. In Your holy and powerful name we pray, Jesus. Amen.

For Discussion

1. Read John 19:19–22. John is the only writer to record
   the three languages on the sign mounted above the
   Cross. In his day, Hebrew was the language of the
   religious people, Latin was the language of the Roman
   empire, and Greek was the language of the common
   people. What might John have been emphasizing by
   mentioning the use of the different languages?

2. Read Exodus 12:46 and Isaiah 53:9. Record the spe-
   cific prophecies mentioned in those passages that are
   fulfilled in John 19:33–38. Why do you think God
   enmeshed so many prophetic details in Jesus's story?
   Explain any impact their fulfillment has on you.

3. In John 19:40, Joseph and Nicodemus prepare Jesus's
   body for burial by anointing Him with spices. One of
   the burial spices used in their day was myrrh. Can you
   find a Scripture reference to another day in Jesus's life
   when He was gifted with myrrh? Record it here along
   with any takeaway you might have about it being
   present at both scenes.

CHAPTER TWENTY

Keep Believing to Have Life

D ear John,

We're at chapter twenty of the study I'm writing on your gospel, and it's got me all up in my emotions. I've been looking forward to writing on this part of your message for a long time now. I thought I'd be excited to be here, and I am, but I'm also terribly nervous. I really want to get this part right (or as close to it as I can come.) Your closing words in this chapter have spurred me on so many times to believe, and keep believing, in the face of all the questions and doubts that can assail a person in this world. To quote you, John, you said it's in believing that we find life in Jesus's name. I understand you to be emphasizing the importance of believing as the present-tense form of the word "believe," and I couldn't agree more. Faith built on a past-tense experience has no life to offer us in present-tense turmoil. That's more of my experience talking. I remember one such time in my life when one of my dearest friends was facing back-to-back tragedies that threatened everything I had ever believed.

To say the Christmas season was proving painfully hard for Debbie's whole family would be a gross understatement. Seven months earlier her handsome, athletic, teenage son, Wade, had been killed in a car wreck and her family's lives had changed forever.

But on this particular day, she had shaken out of her grief long enough to venture out of the house for the first time to do some Christmas shopping with her sister-in-law, Laura. I'd been so proud of her that morning when she shared her plans with me over the phone. It had been a long, hard season for her, but it looked like Debbie was finding her way back to us.

But now—just a few hours later—I was at Pecanland Mall with other friends and family members, searching for Debbie to break more devastating news none of us could have seen coming.

It's hard to relive it, and yet every detail is etched in my brain: The mall was loud and overwhelming. Nearby, at the North Pole, a long line of eager children waited for their turn on Santa's lap. (I'll explain the Santa thing later, John. It's not relevant.) Busy shoppers whizzed by toting heavy bags. Over the intercom, a voice repeatedly asked Debbie B. Fortenberry to please come to the information desk. I remember staring blankly at several guards as they asked me for a description of my friend so they could help find her.

I wanted to help, but all I could remember was the grief I'd seen on Debbie's face for the last seven months. *What would she do now?* So Phil took over, describing Debbie as five-foot-six or -seven with sandy blond hair and blue eyes. Meanwhile, I frantically scanned the crowd.

Suddenly, I saw her. She was fifty or sixty feet away in a sea of people, but they all faded away. She was coming! We'd found her.

But then it hit me: I was going to have to tell her. Up until that very moment, finding Debbie had consumed me, crowding out any realization that once she was found, I'd be responsible for breaking the horrible news that would bring her world crashing down around her. Again.

I watched her approach, her face twisted into one large question mark—her eyes demanding to know "What now?" I desperately wanted time to stop while I figured out what to do. *Oh, God,* I thought, *where were You? Where are You?*

And then Debbie was standing right in front of me, anxious to know why she'd been paged, panic mounting in her voice. Debbie knew these looks on our faces. I stalled by asking where Laura was, then summoned the strength to tell her there'd been an accident and we needed to go home.

Debbie's eyes searched my face, and I looked to Phil for help. *How do people do this?* I wanted to find Laura and get Debbie out of this mall and home to her people before she heard the new horrible truth, but it wasn't going to happen. She already had both hands on my shoulders and was demanding answers.

"What, Shellie? Tell me!" Debbie pummeled me with questions. Who was it? Was it her husband, David? Was he hurt? She was beginning to cry. I fumbled my answers, putting off the inevitable. *No, it wasn't David. Oh, Debbie, how do I tell you?*

"Let's find Laura," I pleaded.

"No! Tell me now, or I'm not moving."

It's hard to remember how long we went on that way. Seconds? Minutes? The unavoidable became obvious. I finally found myself telling Debbie that Justin, her oldest child, a freshman at Louisiana State University, had been shot outside his apartment. I told her he'd been taken to the hospital there and we needed to go. I wanted to leave it there until I could get her home.

I knew Jut Jut, as she called him, had been calling several times a day ever since his little brother had died to check on his mom and tell her he loved her. I knew the strength and comfort his calls had been giving her. *God, how could You let this happen to her? Again?*

Debbie's voice trembled. She asked about her husband. I told her David was already headed to Baton Rouge, to Justin, but she had family and friends waiting for her at home. Everything I was saying was true; everything I was not saying was written on my face.

"He's dead, isn't he? Tell me, Shellie, I'm not going anywhere until you do! Tell me—Justin's dead, isn't he?" Debbie yelled as she pounded on my chest.

This was really happening. I was out of time and forced to nod my head. Phil and I caught Debbie as she slumped to the ground. In between wails, an incredulous look came over her face as her mind struggled to make sense of this fresh nightmare.

"Are you trying to tell me that I don't have any boys? Is that what you're saying?"

I was vaguely aware that a huge crowd had gathered. I wanted to scream at them to go away. Out of my peripheral vision I saw my own twelve-year-old son standing to our side, looking forlorn and helpless. I wanted to reach for him, but I knew I couldn't. Not then. Through her sobs Debbie asked if we'd found Sarah. *Oh my God*, I thought, *Sarah is here?! She'll have to know, too!* I wondered what would happen to the grieving fifteen-year-old when she heard that she had lost another big brother—her last big brother. I knelt with Debbie on the mall floor, rocking her in my arms as she moaned.

The truth is, John, my faith in God wasn't really tested when Debbie lost her first son. I was ready with my Christian support. I pulled from my knowledge of the Bible and tried to help her heal. I prayed for Debbie and with her. We talked, cried, and grieved together. Wade's death was tragic, but I understood that bad things happen, and in my heart believed God was still good. But seven months later, when God allowed Justin to be killed in a freak accident at the hands of his best friend, everything I thought I knew about Him was shaken.

The way I saw it, Debbie had just managed to pull herself up and begin dusting the dirt off her knees when God allowed her to be knocked down again. I didn't know this God. He seemed cruel. This time when Debbie turned to me, any spiritual solace I offered was faked. I said what she needed to hear but it all came from my head, never crossing my cold heart. I thought surely I was losing my mind as I counseled her to cling to the Lord, because I was pushing Him away, and I knew it. I continued to go to church with my family, but nothing penetrated the deep freeze in my spirit.

I felt fractured and insecure. I didn't want my teenagers to be angry with God, and I still wanted them to believe. I just wasn't sure I still did—at least not in the way I had before. Silently I fumed at God, not sure He was even there to listen. Debbie had been so faithful to testify of His sustaining grace through her first son's death. *Hadn't she passed?* I railed. *Hadn't she done good enough for You?*

I'll never forget the day I asked Debbie if she was angry with God. She looked surprised. Shaking her head adamantly she answered, "Never! It hurts something horrible—but the Lord holds me up. I couldn't make it without Him. Every day I ask Him to help me make it one more day. The next day, I thank Him for the day before and ask Him for one more. I can't explain it, but I can't be angry with Him." *Well, that's fine,* I thought. *But I'm furious.*

I fell into a morning routine after that awful day in the mall: I'd stand in the shower, letting the steaming water run over me while I cried and went through the motions of something as close to prayer as I could come. When the hot water ran cold, I'd dry my tears and my body and shut my feelings off until the following day and the next shower. One day, with the water beginning to chill and the same questions chasing each other in my head, I said half to myself and half to the ceiling, "I don't have any peace. I don't trust You anymore, and I wonder if I ever will."

Moments later, I felt a warmth begin to thaw my heart. I didn't hear audible words from Heaven, but I began to understand that I would have peace again—but it wouldn't come because I got all the answers I thought I needed. Somehow, I was being assured my peace would return—only this time my faith would not be in my supposed ability to understand God, but in God Himself. I couldn't prove it, John. I still can't. But I heard God that day. It made me ache to hear Him again, and it made me look for Him in a different, deeper way than I ever had before.

As time passed, I couldn't deny the supernatural healing taking place in Debbie. She taught me a lot about grieving. When she had a bad day, she grieved. And I mean *grieved*! She cried and wailed and looked at pictures until she was exhausted and her emotions were spent. Then she'd put a smile on her face and embrace life again, until the grief built up and overflowed again. Debbie taught

me to treasure life. I watched her help Sarah move past the tragedies. Instead of smothering her last child, Debbie encouraged her
to reach for her dreams. Debbie's example taught me not to live in
fear. Debbie also loves people! She seems to feel for them more than
the rest of us do. I've watched her reach out to other parents who've
lost children, using her own experience to help them through their
grief. It was impossible to watch Debbie and not see the God who
was sustaining her.

I had so wanted to comfort Debbie, to help her heal. Instead,
Debbie's love for people and her reliance on God was healing the
rift in *my* heart. Slowly, steadily, my peace returned. I will always
be grateful to my friend. She helped me rediscover the healing,
loving God I had once known. During the darkest days of her life,
Debbie showed me the way back to God.

That was many years ago. My testimony is that I've since found
Him faithful to reveal Himself to me time and again. Sometimes it
is through prayer, and other times it's through His people. Most
often though, He speaks to me through His Word. Of course, I've
had plenty of opportunities to keep believing. We all do. It's hard
to let go of all the questions and trust God, isn't it? You were open
enough with your own experience for me to know that you and the
other disciples had a hard time with it, too. I can't begin to imagine
what all you know now that you didn't know then. One day our
faith will also become sight, yes? Until then, love on Jesus for me.
I'll talk to you later.

Hugs,
Shellie

PS: I asked Debbie for permission to share her story. She
couldn't have been more delighted with the idea. Her exact words

were, "Why wouldn't I let you tell the world how God held us up?" And then in a later text she added, "I'm truly blessed beyond measure." Isn't that amazing, John? I saved her message. It captures what only God can do in and through those who believe and keep believing.

Dear Reader,

Jesus's twelve disciples sat at His feet absorbing His teachings for three years. They ministered with Him and witnessed miracle after miracle. At the end, they watched as He was betrayed by Judas, endured a farce of a trial, was tortured, hung on a cross, died, and buried in a borrowed tomb—all fulfilling countless treasured ancient prophecies to the letter. And yet, in this last chapter, we'll focus on how the disciples were coming ever closer to a stronger belief in who Jesus was, is, and who He will forever be, and why that can be an encouragement to us. Let's read the first passage together.

> [1] Now on the first day of the week Mary Magdalene came early to the tomb, while it was still dark, and saw the stone already removed from the tomb. [2] So she ran and came to Simon Peter and to the other disciple whom Jesus loved, and said to them, "They have taken the Lord from the tomb, and we do not know where they have put Him." [3] So Peter and the other disciple left, and they were going to the tomb. [4] The two were running together; and the other disciple ran ahead, faster than Peter, and came to the tomb first; [5] and he stooped to look in, and saw

the linen wrappings lying there; however he did not go in. [6] So Simon Peter also came, following him, and he entered the tomb; and he looked at the linen wrappings lying there, [7] and the face-cloth which had been on His head, not lying with the linen wrappings but folded up in a place by itself. [8] So the other disciple who had first come to the tomb also entered then, and he saw and believed. [9] For they did not yet understand the Scripture, that He must rise from the dead. (John 20)

I need you to understand that I don't point out the disciples' slowness to believe to belittle them. On the contrary, I've mentioned it throughout this study, and we'll camp there now for the very reason John was so open about recording it: to help us believe and keep believing, too!

We can take encouragement from every step of the disciples' faith journey to keep moving forward in our own. We can be grateful to the good apostle for humble admissions like "they did not yet understand," because these slow-of-heart men are the same ones who became giants of the faith. Later, the majority would become martyrs and water Gospel seeds with their own blood. And yet, they all had to grow in faith to stand against opposition. We can answer that same call.

It tickles me to know that John outran Peter, but Peter out-dared John. John stopped at the entrance of Jesus's tomb. He only found the nerve to go in after Peter did. Which is when, once again at the risk of being redundant, we note John's confession that he took in the scene and believed. What he saw added to his faith, increasing what he already knew. Peter, who had so recently denied Jesus, had clearly repented. He was following hard after Jesus again, and we see his courage strengthening his friend, John. This is what we can do for each other. Your pursuit of Christ bolsters mine!

> [19] Now when it was evening on that day, the first day of the week, and when the doors were shut where the disciples were together due to fear of the Jews, Jesus came and stood in their midst, and said to them, "Peace be to you." [20] And when He had said this, He showed them both His hands and His side. The disciples then rejoiced when they saw the Lord. [21] So Jesus said to them again, "Peace be to you; just as the Father has sent Me, I also send you." [22] And when He had said this, He breathed on them and said to them, "Receive the Holy Spirit. [23] If you forgive the sins of any, their sins have been forgiven them; if you retain the sins of any, they have been retained."
>
> [24] But Thomas, one of the twelve, who was called Didymus, was not with them when Jesus came. [25] So the other disciples were saying to him, "We have seen the Lord!" But he said to them, "Unless I see in His hands the imprint of the nails, and put my finger into the place of the nails, and put my hand into His side, I will not believe."

Poor Thomas. I don't believe he deserved the nickname Doubting Thomas. After all, Scripture didn't give him that name, the Church did. I think it should've been Honest Thomas, if

anything. If Thomas is the poster child for not believing unless he
sees, we've all been in that picture with him.

> [26] Eight days later His disciples were again inside, and
> Thomas was with them. Jesus came, the doors having
> been shut, and stood in their midst and said, "Peace be
> to you." [27] Then He said to Thomas, "Place your finger
> here, and see My hands; and take your hand and put it
> into My side; and do not continue in disbelief, but be a
> believer." [28] Thomas answered and said to Him, "My
> Lord and my God!" [29] Jesus said to him, "Because you
> have seen Me, have you now believed? Blessed are they
> who did not see, and yet believed."

Circle that last sentence. Highlight it. Draw some happy faces
around it! That's us, my friend. We can choose that blessing as our
own. We don't yet see the scars on His hands and the print of the
spear in His side, but Jesus promises that we are blessed because
we believe anyway.

> [30] So then, many other signs Jesus also performed in the
> presence of the disciples, which are not written in this
> book; [31] but these have been written so that you may
> believe that Jesus is the Christ, the Son of God; and that
> by believing you may have life in His name.

Let's talk about what it means to have life in Jesus's name. As
we said earlier, in the Bible, a name is the revelation of who a person

is—their nature and their attributes. When the Lord was teaching His disciples to pray, He said to pray in this way: "Our Father, who art in heaven. Hallowed be thy name." "Hallow" means "to revere, to respect." Jesus was telling us to honor and revere all that has been revealed to us about His Father and ours.

In a similar way, John is telling us that we can have life in Jesus's name by believing (present tense) in all that Jesus is and everything that Has been revealed to us about Him. As surely as our initial belief in Jesus gives us eternal life, our ongoing choice to believe in Him in spite of everything this world throws at us gives us overcoming life. Pick up your Bible and hold it to your chest. God's Word reveals Jesus to us, and Jesus is the express image of the invisible God. He is God's revelation to us, and what has been revealed is more than enough, in the face of all questions or doubts, to give life to all who believe and keep believing. Why? Because He is present as we continue to believe, and His indwelling Spirit is life. Let's pray.

Dear Jesus,

Help us to not fall back when we are discouraged and confused and we don't know where You are or what You're doing. We see in Your Word that it is okay if we are falling forward, not quite sure of where You're going, but determined to go with You. Thank You for allowing us to see Your patience with those who followed You then. It encourages us to believe in Your longsuffering ways with us now. Help us to keep coming to You, even when our faith is weak and we understand only in part. Give us a growing, persistent, daring faith, that we might embolden other believers in their faith!

We thrill to Your blessing in John 20:29. We claim that blessing as our own, for we do not yet see You with our eyes, Lord, but we believe in our hearts. When we are weary of this world and our faith is being attacked from all sides, remind us of these sweet words of affirmation from Your own lips.

Lord, jar us awake when we are dozing in our faith and relying on any past tense experience instead of actively seeking You and what You're doing in our lives today. We believe we can have life by present-tense, ongoing belief in Your Name, in all that You are and all You have revealed to us. In this Name—this Name that is above all others—we pray, Jesus. Amen.

For Discussion

1. Read John 20:1–18 and Galatians 3:28. Mary was given the privilege of being the first person to see Jesus after His resurrection. Do you think it's because she stayed behind? Could it have anything to do with Galatians 3:28? Both? Please journal your thoughts.

2. Read Matthew 27:46. Now, record John 20:17 and circle the words "my" and "your." This is the first time Jesus refers to His followers as brothers. In your own words, explain the significance of this message He wanted Mary to take to them.

3. Read John 20:22, Genesis 2:7, and 2 Corinthians 5:17. What connection do you see between these verses? Explain.

CHAPTER TWENTY-ONE

Fact-Check the World with the Word

D ear John,
Did you know commentators consider the last chapter of your gospel an epilogue? That's because Chapter 20 sounds like you're wrapping up your manuscript and then—surprise, you come back with more! Although some have suggested Chapter 21 was written by another author entirely, the general consensus is that the extra material was a late addition, but you're still the one who penned it. For what it's worth, John, I believe you wrote it, and I think you would've kept right on writing had Holy Spirit not led you to rest your quill. Granted, I could be projecting here because I'm not at all ready to end this study. Nothing new there. I'm used to feeling like I've got more I want to say or need to say about Jesus when it's time to close a message or finish a writing project, but those emotions seem even stronger with this one.

Why? Because your gospel has taught me to keep running hard after Jesus even when my spiritual knees are still skinned and bloody from my latest fall. You've helped me believe that Jesus doesn't turn away from me when I'm fearful and discouraged, He reaches for me to strengthen my faith. Praise Him. Poring over your words convinced me that my doubts don't bar me from His Presence or disqualify me from requesting fresh resources for the battle! Sharing the struggles that you and the other disciples had in believing Jesus, and how often He did and said things to bolster your faith—this has taught me to resist the temptation to try to hide from Jesus when unbelief is assailing me.

I know now to humble myself in those moments, to be open before the One who already sees me and trust my Keeper to keep me! These are the transformative truths I wanted to share with others in these pages, to help them believe and keep believing. Only the Father knows to what extent I've succeeded. But the mention of truth prompts me to get on with this last letter. Right now, it feels like the clock is ticking in more ways than one.

There's no easy way to get into this, so I'll just say it. We've got a mess on our hands down here, and the root of it all is the enemy's unceasing assault on God's Word. I realize the devil has been trying to cast doubt on God's Word since he first whispered his lies to Eve, but he seems to be making some wicked headway in our day. I'm old enough to remember when God's Word was widely respected, John. Even those who didn't read the Bible and had zero intention of obeying it largely accepted Scripture as truth. Sadly, many now consider truth to be fluid, and they equate it with personal opinion. It's "his truth," "her truth," and "their truth," which means wrong can be right and right can be wrong according to whoever is evaluating it. No doubt you can imagine the far-ranging consequences this is having on our society, but let me give you a wide-angle take on how it relates to our present conversation.

As I've alluded in previous chapters, the public square has become a minefield, and one sure way to light a fuse in these contentious days is to testify to Jesus as the Way, the Truth, and the Life. It's somewhat acceptable to believe that Jesus is *a* way to God, as long as one doesn't insist He is *the* Way. Anyone daring to contend that Jesus is the only avenue sinful man has to be reconciled to Holy God is said to be intolerant and possibly even a threat to national security. (The more things change, the more they stay the same. Right, John?) This indignation toward the Gospel is a vivid reminder that Scripture refers to Jesus as the rock of offense and God's stumbling stone. The world insists that there are many paths to God. No need to hesitate between the choices. "Just choose one that fits," they say. "All religions lead to God."

In loving contrast, God made Jesus a stumbling block, meaning no one can accidentally miss Him! Oh, how I love that. People have to trip over Jesus proclaiming Himself to be the Way and persist in their disbelief on the way to eternal punishment. What grace, what marvelous grace. I'm praying we, the Church, will count the cost of continuing to speak about Jesus to lost souls and consider it wholly worth it, for surely there is no good news without Him. So long for now, John. And thanks again for showing us the Light.

Hugs,
Shellie

Dear Reader,

I've long thought of John's epilogue as his answer to the "what now?" mindset. Jesus turned the world upside down at the Cross and simultaneously upended the disciples' individual lives. What did the future hold for them now? What should they do with what they knew? I believe we ask similar questions when we come to faith, and the chaos of our times is stirring them up and magnifying the uncertainty. The disciples' temporary response to their "what now?" was to go fishing. They knew fishing; it was familiar. Perhaps it felt safe. We get that, don't we?

As the chapter opens, the disciples are returning to shore empty-handed when the resurrected Christ appears and tells them where to cast their nets for a haul. Interestingly enough, they don't recognize Him until their nets begin straining under the catch. So they didn't recognize Jesus when He began speaking, but were eager to greet Him once He met their needs? Ouch. Jesus had a fire going and breakfast waiting. He invited the men to add their fish to what He had prepared and dine with Him. Let's turn to the Word and pick up after the meal. It's about to get very uncomfortable for Peter.

[15] Now when they had finished breakfast, Jesus said to Simon Peter, "Simon, son of John, do you love Me more than these?" He said to Him, "Yes, Lord; You know that I love You." He said to him, "Tend My lambs." [16] He said to him again, a second time, "Simon, son of John, do you love Me?" He said to Him, "Yes, Lord; You know that I love You." He said to him, "Shepherd My sheep." [17] He said to him the third time, "Simon, son of John, do you love Me?" Peter was hurt because He said to him the

third time, "Do you love Me?" And he said to Him,
"Lord, You know all things; You know that I love You."
Jesus said to him, "Tend My sheep. [18] Truly, truly I tell
you, when you were younger, you used to put on your
belt and walk wherever you wanted; but when you grow
old, you will stretch out your hands and someone else will
put your belt on you, and bring you where you do not
want to go." [19] Now He said this, indicating by what kind
of death he would glorify God. And when He had said
this, He said to him, "Follow Me!" (John 21)

I wrote about that exchange between Peter and Jesus in my
book *Finding Deep and Wide*, so I won't repeat the entirety here.
In a nutshell, Jesus restored a disgraced Peter to fellowship. Peter—
who corrected Jesus, snoozed when He asked him to pray, and
attacked the opposition in his own strength instead of waiting for
Jesus's instruction—this Peter was restored. (Hello, Shellie.)

Before the eyes of Peter's peers and while simultaneously
answering all of their "what now?" questions, we find Jesus
instructing Peter to feed others out of the mutual love the two of
them shared. Malnourished disciples too lazy or indifferent to live
by opening the Bible and feasting on the Truth of God's Word will
always be powerless and unfruitful in reaching a lost world. That's
a tragedy in itself, but neglecting God's Word has other repercus-
sions. It leaves believers vulnerable to the enemy's deception and
unable to discern Truth.

Did you ever play a game called Telephone or Pass the Message
when you were a kid? We did. The rules were simple. Players gathered
in a line or formed a circle. The first child started a message down the

line by whispering it into the ear of the player next to him or her. That person repeated the communication to the next player, and on it went. The fun came once the message made its way around the entire group. At that point the first kid would repeat the message aloud, as it originated, before the last kid revealed the garbled version that reached the end of the line. The distortion between the two was always good for a laugh. In our last passage, John the Writer shares a curious story that reminds me of that childhood game, but with eternally significant consequences. Take it in and then meet me below.

> [20] Peter turned around and saw the disciple whom Jesus loved following them—the one who also had leaned back on His chest at the supper and said, "Lord, who is the one who is betraying You?" [21] So Peter, upon seeing him, said to Jesus, "Lord, and what about this man?" [22] Jesus said to him, "If I want him to remain until I come, what is that to you? You follow Me!" [23] Therefore this account went out among the brothers, that that disciple would not die; yet Jesus did not say to him that he would not die, but only, "If I want him to remain until I come, what is that to you?"

We've just been given the antidote to living in a world where facts are manipulated and it's hard to know who to believe. It is vital that we stay grounded in the truth of God's Word. We can't judge "breaking news" apart from it. Notice that John said a rumor went around that one disciple wouldn't die, but "that wasn't what Jesus had said." The Bible doesn't say whether the rumor got started by one of those who were actually present at the time or someone else, but somewhere down the line it got twisted in the retelling. And here's a detail we can't afford to miss: it was being retold "among the brothers," meaning the believers were the ones repeating it! John corrects the misinformation with Jesus's own words, teaching us that Scripture is our unwavering, unchanging foundation.

We're called to stand on gospel Truth and carry it into the world even now, when rumors spread at breakneck speed and everyone chooses their own set of facts. We can't afford to think that we are impervious to the enemy's lies and distortions. The disciples weren't, and we aren't. Our only hope of avoiding deceit is to return over and again to Truth Himself. Holy Spirit is ever-present to give us discernment when we fact-check the world by the Word instead of fact-checking the Word by the world!

Having corrected that record, John closes his gospel much as he opened it: by sharing his unabashed awe of Jesus and celebrating His work among men. Our beloved disciple has a parting "Ta da!" in his big finish that fuels my hunger to know more of Jesus no matter how many times I read it.

> [24] This is the disciple who is testifying about these things and wrote these things, and we know that his testimony is true. [25] But there are also many other things which Jesus did, which, if they were written in detail, I expect that even the world itself would not contain the books that would be written.

John had penned the firsthand account of Jesus's life that he was tasked with documenting, but he can't resist alluding to the wealth of stories he could yet tell. And isn't that how it should be?

I like to remind anyone with ears to hear that whatever you and I know of Jesus, there is more. There is always more. May we stay in hot pursuit of Him together.

Dear Jesus,

Bind our wandering hearts to You! When we take our eyes off of You, we are easily overwhelmed by the state of our world. Things we never thought could happen do, and fear of what might be coming next stalks us. We know You have not given us a spirit of fear, but one of power, love, and sound mind (2 Timothy 1:7). We stand on that promise. It is good medicine for what ails us. We can experience peace in the turmoil because You are our "what now?"!

We aim to feast on Your Word and seek Your company in prayer. We want to answer Your call and tend Your sheep out of the relationship we have with You. Would You strengthen us in these commitments? Would You grant us a hunger that can't be filled and a thirst that can't be slaked by anything less than Your Presence in our daily lives? Knowing this is Your desire, we give You thanks even now for answering these requests.

We are guilty of complaining about the prevalence of relative truth that is no truth at all, but we shouldn't be surprised. You told us a spirit of delusion would come upon the earth. Truth hasn't become elusive simply because man offers so many imitations of it. Truth can still be known because You are Truth, and You desire to reveal Yourself to Your people. Help us seek You with all of our hearts, souls, and minds, that we might be able to walk in Truth and lead lost souls to their Savior. Jesus, it's in Your Precious and Matchless Name that we pray. Amen.

For Discussion

. . . .

1. Read John 20:14 and Luke 24:13–35. In those accounts, just as in the beginning of this chapter, it's noted that believers didn't recognize Jesus immediately. Do you think Jesus looked different after the resurrection, or do you think there could be another reason they didn't recognize Him? What might that be, and could there be a lesson for us here?

2. Read Matthew 26:69–74, Mark 14:66–72, and Luke 22:55–62. Record any similarities you notice in the story of Peter denying Jesus that you see in this chapter when Jesus restores him to fellowship and purposes him for ministry. Put yourself in Peter's shoes. How do you think these similarities felt to him? What do you think the purpose for them might have been?

3. Spend a moment thinking about your strongest takeaway or takeaways from this Bible study of John, and journal them on the back of this page. Length isn't important; sincerity is the goal. If you'd like to share your thoughts with me, I'll be waiting at: writeshellie@gmail.com.

Studying with you has brought much joy to my soul. Until next time.

Hugs,
Shellie

Seizing the Good Life

I can't earn
manage or
protect
the good life
but I can seize it
over and again
by filtering
the bad
the good
and the hard
through
the Truth—
Jesus *is* the good life.

Acknowledgements

Acknowledging those who helped get this book into readers' hands is a formidable undertaking. I set out feeling sure I'll fall short, but I refuse to let that familiar feeling stop me from trying.

To Greg Johnson, thanks for being my agent and friend. You're dearly valued in both roles.

Many thanks to Tim Peterson and the Salem Books team, including Jennifer Hoff, Karla Dial, Kim Lilienthal, and Julie Jayne. It's been a blessing to work with each of you.

To my treasured Prayer Circle: Rhonda Perry, Nina McMillian, Susie McKenzie, Cookie Haynes, Denise Sibley, Michelle Renard, Diane Novak, Jeanie Pinkston, Betty Lacey, Deanna Jordan, Ella Brunson Pogue, Tiffany Olson, Karen Lingo, and Janet Wade. Thank you for allowing me to message you whenever I sat down to write this book, and for diligently petitioning the throne on my behalf. May your reward be even greater intimacy with our good, good Father.

To Stephanie Thornton, many thanks to you for the beautiful cover. You knocked it out of the park yet again!

To my parents, my kids, and my grandkids, thanks for understanding when Keggie time has to be sacrificed for writing time.

To my precious husband, known to my readers as The Beloved Farmer. Thank you, Phil. I know full well you're the better half of this team and I'd never be able to write, travel, and speak without your unwavering support. I long for everyone else to recognize your role in this ministry, but I content myself with the knowledge that you don't need the kudos and never have.

And to my Jesus, who knows me through and through and loves me still. Please read the gratitude in my heart, for these words will fall short of expressing it. Thank you for redeeming this woman from an empty manner of living and ever calling her closer still. You are everything.

Connect with Shellie

I truly enjoy connecting with readers. I'd love for you to find me on Facebook, Twitter, Instagram, and Pinterest. You can also e-mail me (writeshellie@gmail.com) or send an actual letter to:

610 Schneider Lane, Lake Providence, LA 71254

Are you part of a book club? I'd be happy to connect with your group. Contact me and we'll make it happen. After more than a decade in radio, I've moved to podcasting from my home here on the banks of Lake Providence. *The Story Table* podcast can be found on your favorite podcasting platform. You're also warmly invited to subscribe to my lifestyle website (shelliet.com) where you'll have FREE access to all my latest recipes and find booking information to have me speak to your church group or organization. Regardless of how you choose to connect, do reach out and let's seek Jesus together, forever. He is worthy!

More from Shellie

A STORYTELLING COOKBOOK

Hungry is a Mighty Fine Sauce

SHELLIE RUSHING TOMLINSON

Chasing Jesus Six Days from Sunday

Devotions
FOR THE
Hungry Heart

Shellie Rushing Tomlinson

Finding Deep & Wide

Stop Settling for the Life You Have and
Live the One Jesus Died to Give You

SHELLIE RUSHING TOMLINSON

H E A R T
W I D E
O P E N

TRADING MUNDANE FAITH
FOR AN EXUBERANT LIFE WITH JESUS

SHELLIE RUSHING TOMLINSON

Rocking It
GRAND

— 18 WAYS TO BE A —
GAME-CHANGING GRANDMA

Chrys Howard and
Shellie Rushing Tomlinson

FOCUS ON FAMILY

Suck Your Stomach In & Put Some Color On!

What Southern Mamas
Tell their Daughters that
the Rest of Y'all Should
Know Too

Shellie Rushing
Tomlinson

Host of All Things Southern

"Laugh-out-loud funny."
—Jeff Foxworthy

Sue Ellen's Girl Ain't Fat, She Just Weighs Heavy

The Belle of All Things Southern
Dishes on Men, Money, and Not
Losing Your Midlife Mind

Shellie Rushing Tomlinson

National Bestselling Author of Suck Your Stomach In & Put Some Color On!